THE KING
IS DEAD

ALSO BY SUZANNAH LIPSCOMB

A Journey Through Tudor England

THE KING IS DEAD

The Last Will and Testament of Henry VIII

SUZANNAH LIPSCOMB

PEGASUS BOOKS
NEW YORK LONDON

THE KING IS DEAD

Pegasus Books Ltd.
148 West 37th Street, 13th Floor
New York, NY 10018

First Pegasus Books cloth edition December 2016

Interior design by Maria Fernandez

ISBN: 978-1-68177-254-7

10 9 8 7 6 5 4 3 2 1

Printed in the United States of America
Distributed by W. W. Norton & Company, Inc.

For the first History cohort to graduate from
New College of the Humanities—
Francesca, Samuel, Frances,
Joshua, Paula,
Jonathan, Alfred and Max—
with great affection, pride, and admiration.

"Let's talk of graves, of worms, and epitaphs . . .
Let's choose executors and talk of wills . . .
For God's sake, let us sit upon the ground
And tell sad stories of the death of kings . . ."

—William Shakespeare,

Richard II, Act III, Scene II

Contents

Foreword

Henry VIII's last will and testament is one of the most intriguing and contested documents in British history. Given special legal and constitutional significance by the 1536 and 1544 Acts of Succession, which allowed Henry to nominate his successor in his last will, it is exceptional among English royal wills. For Henry VIII, the monarch so renowned—or notorious—for remarrying in pursuit of a male heir, the succession was his abiding obsession until the very end.

Throughout the sixteenth century, Henry VIII's will was called upon to determine the course of history. On the accession of Henry's nine-year-old son as Edward VI, Henry's will was used both to justify government by a regency council under the increasingly authoritarian sway of Edward Seymour, Duke of Somerset, as "Lord Protector of England," and then to warrant the dissolution of Somerset's protectorate in October 1549. Four years later, the will was overruled—if temporarily—to divert the succession to Edward VI's cousin, the Protestant Lady Jane Grey. During Elizabeth I's reign, it was deemed invalid by those who supported Mary, Queen of Scots' claim to the English throne.

Despite these challenges, however, until Elizabeth's own death and the accession of James VI of Scotland as England's James I in 1603, the sequence of childless English monarchs over the previous half-century meant that the line of succession as laid out in Henry VIII's will came to pass.

In the centuries since, historians have disagreed vehemently over the will's intended meaning, its authenticity and validity, and the circumstances of its creation. One school of thought—represented by such great names of Tudor history as Geoffrey R. Elton, David Starkey and John Guy—has argued that it was the product of a conspiracy staged by an "evangelical" or proto-Protestant faction at court seeking to advance religious reform, led by Edward Seymour (at that time Earl of Hertford) and Sir William Paget. These historians assert that the will remained unsigned until Henry was on his deathbed; that, in the month between Henry drawing up its final form in December 1546 and his death on January 28, 1547, Hertford and Paget added clauses enabling their subsequent assumption of power; and that the will was hurriedly stamped as Henry lay dying, to ensure its legitimacy. Having maneuvered to guarantee the dominance of religious reformers on the Privy Council—which meant destroying the religious conservatives who stood in their way—the evangelicals, it is argued, were then perfectly poised to attain control of the government at the accession of Edward VI.[1]

In this book, I disagree wholeheartedly with this interpretation. Although faction did exist at court, I am convinced that these historians have been too influenced by the sixteenth-century martyrologist John Foxe's estimation of Henry VIII: "according as his counsel was about him, so was [he] led."[2] I believe—by contrast—that until very close to the hour of his death, Henry was clearly directing events.

In the course of my research, I have also discovered that the case for a coup by reformers and for an alteration of the will is based on some notable errors. These are described fully in the narrative that follows, and in its Notes on the Text, but it is worth briefly mentioning here the three main bones of contention.

The first is the assertion that, as Professor Elton put it, "the Privy Council . . . for a crucial month (December 8, 1546 to January 4, 1547) met not at court but in Hertford's town house" and that this locus for their meetings indicates the growing power of the alleged reformist faction at that time.[3] Both fact and conclusion have subsequently been accepted by other historians.[4] But it is a piece of misinformation, deriving from François Van der Delft, the ambassador for the Holy Roman Empire— one of the clearest indications that he sometimes got things wrong—and can be disproved by the minutes of the Privy Council, which show that the Council actually met at Ely Place in Holborn, the townhouse of Sir Thomas Wriothesley.[5] He was not only Henry's lord chancellor but a prominent religious *conservative*. This piece of "evidence," used to imply the domination and manipulation of England's primary organ of government by the reformers as they built their power base, therefore proves nothing of the sort.

More significantly, some historians claim to have, as one put it, "incontrovertible evidence" that the will was altered.[6] They assert that that the will was tampered with after December 1546 and then stamped with Henry VIII's device to reproduce his signature—the "dry stamp"; and they have attempted to prove this by observing that the will lists Sir Thomas Seymour, younger brother of Edward Seymour, as a Privy Councillor, even though he was only appointed as such on January 23, 1547. On this basis, David Starkey has concluded that "armed with this sort of evidence, no modern court would hesitate to overturn Henry's last will and testament."[7] Yet the simple fact is that Thomas Seymour is not listed in this way in the will; rather, he is presented as an assistant to the regency council that Henry planned, a position that did not require prior membership of the Privy Council. Indeed, membership of Henry VIII's Privy Council and the regency council of sixteen named in the will were not coterminous: there were six regency councillors and two other assistants, besides Thomas Seymour, who were not Privy Councillors when the will was drawn up.[8] With the dismantling of this error, the theory that the will was tampered with starts to look structurally unsound, and indeed becomes unsustainable.

Third, and finally, there is the notion that Henry VIII could not bear to think of his impending death, as first alleged by Foxe and taken up by later historians.[9] By contrast, Sir William Paget, the king's close secretary, remembered in February 1547 Henry saying—probably at some point in December—"that he felt himself sickly, and . . . could not long endure," and as a result prepared himself for death by making plans with Paget to provide for the care of his son.[10] It may be that Paget was not a reliable narrator at this juncture; but it seems likely that rather than Henry fearing to speak of his death, those who dared not speak of it were his advisers, because under the Treasons Act of 1534 it was traitorous to imagine the king's death in words.[11] In the face of his mortality, Henry was probably not the ostrich that has been depicted.

◈

Having pointed to these specific points of interpretation, I ought to add that every historian builds on the work of others, as much as he or she questions it. Many historians have brought their excellent logic and profound analysis to bear on the questions I consider here. Their scholarship has illuminated the murky business of unravelling Henry's will, and I owe a debt of thanks to them, and to others besides, whose names appear in this book's Acknowledgements. In adding one more layer to the accumulation of comment and opinion about the circumstances and meaning of Henry VIII's last will and testament, I hope that I, too, have brought a little more light to bear.

SUZANNAH LIPSCOMB
Château de Foncoussières
April 2015
SDG

A Note on Spelling, Dates, and Money

SPELLING

Although I find the curious orthography of the sixteenth century enchanting, in the main text of this book I have modernized spelling and punctuation, and silently expanded contractions, for ease of reading.

The spellings used by the authorities I cite or quote have, though, been retained in the book's endnotes ("Notes on the Text"); and the full, unmodernized, original-spelling version of the will appears as Appendix I.

DATES

The dates are those of the Julian Calendar, which was used in England until 1752, even though most of continental Europe had adopted the Gregorian Calendar in 1582. However, the calendar year is assumed to start on January 1st, rather than on Lady Day (March 25). The date of Henry VIII's death is therefore given as January 28, 1547.

MONEY

English currency in Henry VIII's reign (indeed, until 1971) was made up of pounds, shillings and pence: twenty shillings to the pound sterling, and twelve pence to the shilling.

Twelve pounds, seven shillings and five pence was written "12 l. 7 s. 5 d.," but I have modernized to the better-known form "£12 7s 5d." It was also normal to count in marks, a mark being worth two-thirds of a pound, or 13s 4d. So, 500 marks = roughly £333 4s.

I have not given modern equivalents of sums in the text, because, after inflation, and in an age where we value different commodities, these tend to be rather misleading. The following contemporary facts may, though, provide some useful orientation:

- Nicholas Lentall, a servant to Stephen Gardiner, Bishop of Winchester, received £5 a year in wages, plus "meat, drink and livery," and a £10 annuity.[12]
- Hans Holbein, court painter to Henry VIII, received a salary of £30 a year.
- The average assessed income from lands per annum for the peerage was £873 in 1545.[13]

I

The Death of a King

T here is a strange symmetry to the dates. The founder of the
Tudor dynasty, Henry VII, was born in obscurity on January
28, 1457; his famous, infamous, son died in the profound dark-
ness of a winter's night on the same day ninety years later. He was fifty-five
years old, grossly overweight, and had been plagued for a decade by a terrible running sore on his leg that had recently forced him into the Tudor
equivalent of a wheelchair and a stairlift.[1] He was also still "Henry the
Eighth, by Grace of God, King of England, Ireland and France, Defender
of the Faith, and Supreme Head of the Church of England," and at 2 A.M.
on January 28, 1547, in the thirty-eighth year of his reign, he took his last
breath.

Although he had predicted some weeks earlier that his death might not
be long in coming, only ten days before he died he had been well enough
to meet ambassadors from France and the Holy Roman Empire. Six days
before his death, he had given firm orders to his indefatigable secretary, Sir
William Paget, on a matter of foreign policy.[2] So, while the king's sickness
and bouts of indisposition had long been a familiar reality at court, and

the prospect of his demise therefore always a possibility, the end itself came all of a sudden.

On the evening of January 27, a kind of terror must have gripped his courtiers' hearts. They could see that he was dying and knew therefore that their zealous sovereign needed to prepare his soul to meet his Maker. Yet, an Act passed in Parliament some thirteen years earlier had made it high treason to speak of the king's death.[3] The lion looked old and enfeebled, but there was still every chance that he could swipe at one of them with his ebbing strength; indeed, the unctuous Thomas Howard, 3rd Duke of Norfolk, a recent victim of the king's displeasure, was waiting for his moment on Tower Hill the next morning.

It was Denny who was brave. The "gentle" Sir Anthony Denny, a decade younger than his king, had been made first Chief Gentleman of the Privy Chamber a few months earlier, and he was thought by the Imperial ambassador, François Van der Delft, to be "the most confidential of any of the gentlemen of the Chamber."[4] He was close to Henry, he could be trusted, and perhaps he, above all who clustered around Henry's pained and corpulent body, cared enough about the king's fate to risk his own.

Denny told the king that he was "to man's judgment not like to live" and urged him to prepare himself for death.[5] Henry is said to have replied: "the mercy of Christ is able to pardon me all my sins, though they were greater than they be," demonstrating his keenly felt faith as well as an undiminished sense of his own righteousness—both qualities that had characterized his entire reign.

Denny asked if he would like to have any "learned man"—a priest—with whom to confer, to which Henry responded that he would have Dr. Cranmer, his Archbishop of Canterbury; but to Denny's pressing as to whether he would like him sent for immediately, the king replied that he would first "take a little sleep; and then, as I feel myself, I will advise upon the matter." Optimism to the last. Yet, these were to be Henry's final words.

In sixteenth-century England, there was a very clear sense of what a "good death" involved. It did not mean a peaceful surrender to the grim reaper. It meant wrestling through a spiritual ordeal, as the Devil and his demons tried to prise the immortal soul of the dying person away from God and his angels. The deathbed was a battlefield. And so the medieval Catholic Church, into which Henry VIII had been born, had developed a series of rituals designed to walk the perishing through the valley of deathly shadows. These last rites involved a priest holding a crucifix—depicting the Savior, Jesus Christ, crucified on the Cross—in front of the afflicted, placing a lighted candle in their hands, listening to their final confession and absolving their sins. Then a piece of consecrated bread—bread that had, by the miracle of transubstantiation, become the body of Christ, and which was called the *viaticum* (Latin for "take with you on the journey")—was fed to the dying on the point of death. Finally, the expiring body was anointed with blessed oil in an act of extreme unction, before he or she slipped away.[6]

Henry VIII's last minutes, however, bore little relation to this Catholic good death, and there may be a reason for that. Our account of Henry's death comes from John Foxe, an ardent Protestant who wrote his "Book of Martyrs" (*Acts and Monuments*) during the reign of Elizabeth I. Historians, rightly, are cautious of relying unquestioningly on his narrative. His literary style suggests some invention of dialogue, and he certainly has his heroes and villains. Yet, Foxe's accounts were based largely on the evidence of original documents—to which he stuck mostly faithfully—and on the testimony of individuals, and while he may have been partisan, it seems unlikely that he devised whole episodes without a source.[7] And even if Foxe was inclined to recast Henry VIII as a Protestant, the version he gives us actually tells us something else.

Foxe relates that, after sleeping for a couple of hours Henry woke and realized that his end was approaching. He commanded that Cranmer be sent for, but, delayed on the frozen roads, the messenger took time to reach the archbishop, who then took time to travel to Westminster from his house at Croydon. Too much time. When Cranmer arrived, Henry was unable to speak and perilously close to unconsciousness, but wordlessly stretched out his hand to his faithful servant—the cleric who had annulled Henry's marriage to Katherine of Aragon, who had helped him break with the

Church of Rome, and establish the royal supremacy over the Church of England.

Sensing the urgency, Cranmer did not bother with crucifix or candle or even communion, but simply instructed his sovereign to put his trust in Jesus Christ and charged him to make some sign—with eyes or hands—that he put his faith in the Lord. "Then the king, holding him with his hand, did wring his hand in his as hard as he could," a desperate, impassioned last gesture—let it all not have been in vain—and then he died.[8]

The king may have been dead; but that did not mean Henry VIII was prepared to cede power. His chief instrument of control from beyond the grave was to be his last will and testament.

◈

Henry VIII's will had a special legal importance, unique among royal wills. This is because, back in his *annus horribilis* of 1536, he had faced the situation of having, at the age of forty-five, two children but no heirs.[9] In that year he had had a significant fall from his horse while jousting, which opened up an ulcer in his leg; had faced a major rebellion in the north of the country; had seen his seventeen-year-old son, the illegitimate Henry Fitzroy, Duke of Richmond and Somerset, die; and had faced the devastating allegation that the woman he loved had committed adultery with five men, including her own brother, for which Henry had ordered her execution.

Henry's first wife, Katherine of Aragon, had been the widow of his elder brother Arthur, to whom she had been married for just five months before Arthur's death in 1502. The daughter of illustrious parents, Ferdinand of Aragon and Isabella of Castile, Katherine was six years older than Henry, auburn-haired, highly educated, deeply religious, and resilient, having survived seven difficult years of living in limbo after Arthur's death, separated from her family and uncertain as to her future. She and Henry were married in 1509, soon after his accession, and the king and queen were crowned together.

Sir Anthony Denny (1501–49), as depicted in an engraving based on a Holbein sketch: in the early 1540s, Denny was a friend and patron of the great German artist. Denny was also one of the Chief Gentlemen of the King's Privy Chamber and the man who dared to tell the king to prepare for death. He was named as a regency councillor and executor in Henry VIII's will. *Private Collection / Bridgeman Images.*

What seemed at first a happy marriage was soured by the repeated heartbreak of miscarriages, stillbirths, and infant mortality. One prince, named Henry, born in 1511, died just seven weeks later. Only one child—a daughter named Mary, born in 1516—survived. For the sake of the peace of the country, and to prevent civil war and foreign domination—which were thought to be the consequences of female rule—Henry needed sons. The birth of Henry Fitzroy in 1519 to his mistress, Elizabeth Blount, was of little help; Henry VIII's sons needed to be legitimate, and Fitzroy's birth merely confirmed the king's suspicion that the problem lay not with him, but with his wife. By the 1520s, as Katherine reached her forties, Henry feared that her childbearing days were over.

Several developments now occurred at the same time. First, around 1526, Henry met the woman who was to be the love of his life, Anne Boleyn, and he started to imagine the possibility of children by another wife. Second, according to Henry's speech before the papal court at Blackfriars in 1529, which was convened to judge the validity of his marriage to Katherine, "a certain scrupulosity . . . pricked my conscience . . . which doubt pricked, vexed and troubled so my mind, and so disquieted me, that I was in great doubt of God's indignation."[10] This "scrupulosity" was the pressing concern that his lack of a male heir was an indication that he was being punished by God, and that the pope should never have given him a dispensation to marry his brother's widow, which was explicitly prohibited by Scripture (Leviticus, chapter 18, verse 16 and chapter 20, verse 21).[11] These pricks of conscience seem terribly convenient; but Henry was probably quite genuine in his conviction that his first marriage was a sham. He had an infinite capacity for self-delusion and was a great believer in the letter, rather than the spirit, of the law.

Yet, even if the king was sincerely assured of the righteousness of his position, the matter of getting his marriage annulled, usually such a straightforward affair, was this time anything but. In 1527, when Henry began to press for a "divorce," troops belonging to Charles V, the Holy Roman Emperor, had just sacked Rome, and Pope Clement VII was being held prisoner at his Roman fortress of Castel Sant'Angelo. The response

Anne Boleyn (*c.*1501–36), portrayed in a medal from 1534. It was cast in lead when the queen, Henry VIII's second wife, was thought to be pregnant, and it is the only agreed likeness of Anne from her lifetime. The medal shows her long face and high cheekbones. The date and Anne's motto "The Moost Happi" (The Most Happy) are written on the rim, and the initials A.R. spell out "Anna Regina"—Anne the Queen. *Private Collection / Bridgeman Images.*

that the pope could give to Henry's request to annul his marriage thus depended on what Charles V might have to say about it. Given that Charles happened to be Katherine of Aragon's nephew, it was almost inevitable that he would take her side, and Henry's chances looked slim. The papal court called in London in 1529 to hear the matter was a time-wasting affair, largely scuppered by Katherine herself, who had no intention of being put out to pasture. Henry needed another strategy.

It came from the king's burgeoning sense of his own sovereignty. In the twentieth century, historian J. J. Scarisbrick was so convinced of Henry's growing commitment to this notion that he asserted: "even if there had been no divorce Henry might yet have taken issue with the Church."[12] The claim to sovereignty meant asserting that England was an empire and that English kings had always enjoyed spiritual, as well as political, supremacy in their realm. This, in turn, meant that kings of England had no superior: they were first under God, and needed no approval from the pope, nor from any intermediary to meddle in their communications with the Almighty. What this all added up to was the revelation that the pope had no jurisdiction in the matter of Henry's divorce.

Over the early 1530s, this little acorn of thought gradually developed into the mature oak of the royal supremacy, and through an important series of Acts of Parliament, the "break with Rome" was accomplished. In 1534, it was declared that Henry was, and always had been, the Supreme Head of the Church in England. A year earlier, he had married the witty and cosmopolitan mistress Anne Boleyn, and had had his marriage to Katherine of Aragon annulled—in that order—by his scholarly new Archbishop of Canterbury, Thomas Cranmer.

In September 1533, Anne Boleyn bore him a child—not the longed-for son, but a daughter, Elizabeth. Still, the couple hoped that her evident fertility would soon manifest itself in a blush of boys. It was not, of course, to be. After some false starts, Anne miscarried in early 1536; distressingly, she was far enough along in her pregnancy for the doctors to tell that the fetus was male. She had no opportunity to try again. A few months later, she was faced with charges of adultery, incest, and "conspiring for the king's death" and was beheaded on the morning of May 19, 1536 within the walls of the Tower of London. In the aftermath of this disaster, Henry had his marriage to Anne Boleyn declared void, their daughter Elizabeth was proclaimed illegitimate—and neither did the debacle restore Mary's fortunes, for the king forced his elder daughter to swear that the marriage between her parents had been "incestuous and unlawful" and that she herself was a bastard. After the death of Fitzroy in July 1536, Henry was left with two living children and without a legitimate heir.

This was a perilous position to be in, especially for a king acutely sensitive to the perceived novelty of Tudor rule. While Henry had high hopes that his new, third, wife Jane Seymour might play her part, he needed to make provision for a worst-case scenario. And so, in that terrible year of 1536, a Succession Act was passed in Parliament, which confirmed the illegitimacy of his daughters, disinherited them from the right to claim the throne, and determined that his lawful children by Queen Jane, and by any subsequent wife, would succeed him. In the absence of such issue, however, and not wishing to leave the realm "destitute," the statute instructed the king that he would have "full and plenary power and authority to give, dispose, appoint, assign, declare and limit [the succession], by your letters patents under your great seal or else by your last will made in writing and signed by your most gracious hand."[13]

The king, therefore, had the right to appoint his successor by his will. The Act additionally empowered Henry to designate conditions for the succession and to specify the composition of a regency council should his heir be a minor at the time of his death.

These rights were confirmed in the next Succession Act of 1544. By this time, however, a legitimate son, Prince Edward, had been born to Jane and so was named in this Act as Henry's heir, while Lady Mary and Lady Elizabeth (having lost their titles of "Princess" along with their legitimacy) were reinserted back into the line of succession after Edward and his heirs. Crucially, however—for it would have later ramifications—Henry's two daughters were not legitimized. In the light of this legislation, the king's last will would become a document with fundamental constitutional clout.

It would also be very different to the wills of earlier kings. Henry V, Henry VI, Edward IV, and Henry VII had spent the majority of their wills apportioning estates, and making provision for their souls and for the commonwealth. Henry VIII's will had a different *raison d'être*. It was dedicated, as his life had been, to determining the succession and to ensuring the future of the Tudor dynasty. To do so, it arrogated to itself astonishing and hubristic rights to decide the future of the country as no other royal will before it had attempted to do. It set out precisely what Henry wanted to happen after his death—that is, if we can be confident that it really *did* express the king's desires. Whether or not the will was the creation of the king and truly expressed his volition are the first mysteries to be solved.

2

The Last Decade

I n order to understand the circumstances in which Henry VIII's will was drawn up and appreciate the implications and importance of its contents, it is first necessary to know something of the extraordinary developments of Henry's latter years. Henry's physical degeneration in his last decade was sufficient to make an early death likely, and with it came the necessity of planning for the succession of a minor as heir. The simultaneous degeneration in Henry's character meant that the increasingly tyrannical monarch became ever harder to control. Yet, the religious shifts made (as well as those rebuffed) by Henry's government over these years created fault lines among those seeking to influence the king's will and raised the stakes for those wanting to determine the future of the country.

After the traumas of 1536, Henry's last decade began joyfully. On October 12, 1537, his third wife, the docile Jane Seymour, gave birth to their son at Hampton Court. Prince Edward was christened in the chapel there three days later. Yet it was Jane's death from puerperal sepsis, or childbed fever, two weeks after Edward's birth that rather set the tone of the years to come. Plunged into mourning, and no doubt brimming with self-pity as well as grief, the king famed for his fondness for marriage did not wed again for more than two years.

One of the two activities with which Henry preoccupied himself in those years was hunting. After his accident in January 1536, Henry was never able to joust again, but he could still manage to hunt, as he morphed from an attractive youth into a monstrously obese and prematurely aged man. By 1541, the French ambassador, Charles de Marillac, noted that the king had grown "very stout." Measurements of Henry's armor suggest that his waist had increased from 37 inches to 54 inches in just five years.

Much of the inactivity that led to this weight-gain (coupled, one presumes, with a fair amount of comfort-eating) was due to the unabating pain that Henry suffered throughout the last eleven years of his life. Although a constant ache, the ulcer in his leg, opened up by his fall in January 1536, would flare up from time to time in ravaging waves of pain and fever. In spring and summer 1537, the ulcer prevented Henry from traveling far; he wrote to the Duke of Norfolk that he could not journey to York because "to be frank with you, which you must keep to yourself, a humour has fallen into our legs, and our physicians advise us not to go far in the heat of the day."[1] In 1538 and 1541, for a fortnight at a time, he was in so much pain that, as French Ambassador Louis de Perreau, Seigneur de Castillon, noted, "the humours which had no outlet were like to have stifled him, so that he was sometime without speaking black in the face and in great danger."[2]

Castillon, and Henry himself, understood Henry's condition in the light of the medical knowledge of the day: as an excess of one of the body's four humors (of blood, phlegm, and black and yellow bile). Modern physicians have suggested that Henry suffered from osteomylitis, or a chronic septic infection of the femur, and that these intermittent feverish attacks were caused by septic absorption or clotting of the blood, as in deep vein thrombosis (DVT). Untreated—or at least untreated by modern medicine such as anticoagulants—such clots can lead to a pulmonary embolism. It may be this that finally killed Henry, although kidney disease and heart failure (perhaps together with the swollen legs that are characteristic of oedema or dropsy) may have also been contributors.

Less physically strenuous than hunting, Henry's other main preoccupation at this time was theology: he spent hours meticulously correcting a book of doctrine prepared for him by his bishops.

Twenty years earlier, Martin Luther had started his great rebellion against the Catholic Church by protesting against "indulgences"—certificates that promised time off (one thousand years, ten thousand years, twenty thousand years) from the sufferings of purgatory, and which were issued by the Church in exchange for specific good deeds or the donation of money. Luther soon developed his radical theology, which challenged the Church on every level. He believed that to be made right with God, there was nothing the believer needed to do other than accept the grace of God by faith—the doctrine known as "solifidianism" or "justification by grace through faith alone." No amount of works of charity or good deeds or gifts of money could "buy" one's way into heaven. In addition, Luther believed that the Bible had supreme authority over and above the pronouncements of the Church, and he held to the idea of the "priesthood of all believers": that every believer, graciously assisted by God, could do everything necessary for his or her salvation, without resorting to the panoply of priestly services designed to bridge the gap between God and man. Finally, Luther rejected the idea of purgatory after death—the place for purging the debt of one's sins before the Christian could enter Heaven—as a non-Scriptural fiction. Luther believed that Christ had achieved, on the Cross, everything necessary for salvation.

The consequences of this theological shift were vast. It meant a rejection of prayers to saints and the Virgin Mary, for prayers would instead go direct to God; it meant an end to worship with the aid of relics—those physical remnants of the saints—or the shrines and pilgrimages to house and honor them; it meant a redefinition of the role of the priest, who was no longer needed for confession or absolution. In time, followers of Martin Luther, such as John Calvin, added further layers of interpretation, and by the 1540s, across Europe, there were those—known in England as "sacramentarians"—who would claim that the bread and wine of the Mass did not actually *become* the body and blood of Jesus Christ, nor bore his "real presence" while remaining bread and wine, but instead were just symbols designed for remembrance and thanksgiving (although Luther himself never went that far).

When Henry first broke with the Church of Rome, the Church of England simply constituted a replacement of the pope's authority with that of the king. From 1536 onward, however, Henry started to add a theological dimension to his political reformation. This was far from Lutheran. Henry had hated Luther ever since the German had been very rude about the king in response to Henry's book *Assertio Septum Sacramentorum* (*The Defence of the Seven Sacraments*), which had been a rebuttal of Luther's works. Yet, by 1536, Henry was no longer asserting that there were seven sacraments (the Mass, baptism, marriage, penance, confirmation, ordination, and extreme unction). Instead, in the first doctrinal statement of the Church of England—the Ten Articles, produced in 1536—Henry affirmed that there were only three sacraments (the Mass, baptism, and penance). He defined his idiosyncratic religious position as somewhere between Protestantism and Catholicism: justification was by faith, but faith joined with charitable works, not faith alone; the sacrament of penance—confession to, and absolution by, priests—was essential; and Christ was really present in the bread and wine of the Mass. About purgatory, he was ambivalent, conceding that it was good to pray for the souls of the dead, but that the place where they were was unknown.[3]

One area of theology over which Henry and Luther did agree was that the authority of Scripture was greater than that of the pope. A feature of Henry VIII's reformation was, therefore, the introduction of the Bible in English rather than in Latin, and in September 1538 the government ordered that an English Bible be put in every parish church in the land.

Another key component of Henry's reformation, also initiated in 1536, was the eradication of superstition, idolatry, and hypocrisy. The Royal Injunctions of 1536 (written chiefly, despite the title, by Thomas Cromwell) restricted the use of images in worship and the veneration of the saints, called for the destruction of shrines and commanded an end to the practice of pilgrimage. The dissolution of the monasteries began from a similar impulse—the elimination of corrupt practices in the church. But after the Pilgrimage of Grace, a major rebellion in the north of England for which Henry held monks largely responsible, the motives for the wholesale destruction of monasticism were more murky. Revenge, avarice, and an irrepressible sense that monks' first allegiance was treasonably to the pope led to more than eight hundred religious houses being closed in just four years.

It was a reflection of Henry's particular religious positioning that at Smithfield, in July 1540, he could order the simultaneous hanging, drawing, and quartering of three Roman Catholics—for their commitment to the pope—and the burning at the stake of three "heretics," or reformers, for their belief in the principle of justification by faith through grace alone. When Henry amended his bishops' writings about theology in the years after Jane Seymour's death, he adjusted them to fit a theological worldview that was peculiarly his own.

◈

When Henry did marry again, in 1540, it was an absolute fiasco, mitigated only by the fact that the woman in question, Anne of Cleves, left their abortive union after just a few months with her head intact and with a fair clutch of houses. Everyone else may have thought she was "womanly" and "goodly," but Henry found her "nothing as fair as she hath been reported" and could not bring himself to consummate their marriage. His later tight-lipped report was that when he had felt her breasts and stomach, which he thought unmaidenly, he "had neither will nor courage to proceed any further in other matters."[4]

That he had been required to marry her at all he blamed on his first minister, Thomas Cromwell. Cromwell had been at the heart of Henry's government for six years, operating as his master's eyes, ears, hands, and conscience. That did not preclude getting those hands dirty from time to time. The break with Rome, the tricky foreign relations thereafter, the execution of Anne Boleyn, the reform of the Church, the dissolution of the monasteries—all had been Cromwell's doing, on Henry's command. Yet in 1540, the Cleves affair was the catalyst for Cromwell's destruction, and all his pleading was to no avail. He wrote an understandably impassioned, but fruitless, letter to the king from the Tower of London, signing off "with the quaking hand, and most sorrowful heart, of your most sorrowful subject, and most humble servant, and prisoner . . . I cry mercy, mercy, mercy."[5]

Cromwell's execution changed the nature of England's politics. After his death, no single leading minister rose up to replace him. Instead, from August 1540, the King's Privy Council—officially, "the King's Most Honourable Council Attendant upon his Highness Person"—was formally established as England's primary organ of government. Functioning rather like an executive board, its original nineteen members, appointed by the king, worked collectively, making decisions about issues of governance large and small. As a council, they had full executive authority, advising the king, administering the realm, managing national defence, enforcing law and order, regulating economic affairs, investigating crime, managing Parliament, and issuing proclamations in the king's name. Unsurprisingly, such extensive powers of government took time to administer, and the Council met almost every day, usually at court, moving with the king from palace to palace—though very few members attended every meeting.

If the king's six-month marriage to Anne of Cleves had proved Cromwell's undoing, it had at least yielded one apparent benefit for Henry. The king had identified a girl far more to his liking. In classic style, she was a maid of honor to his current queen, just as Jane had been to Anne Boleyn, and Anne to Katherine of Aragon. Distastefully, Henry married his fifth wife, Catherine Howard, on the same day that Cromwell was beheaded.

Catherine's date of birth is unknown, but we can calculate that she was between sixteen and twenty-four years old, to his forty-nine years. For eighteen months, her youth rejuvenated him. In the end, however, his marriage to Catherine came at great emotional cost to him, and an even greater cost to her. The day after he had ordered public prayers to celebrate

A sketch of Henry VIII, made in 1540, possibly by Holbein's assistants. Dating from seven years before the king's death, the drawing shows the monarch's heavyset face, his eyes appearing to glare malignantly and fixedly at the spectator. *The Print Collector / Getty Images.*

his happiness, Henry's archbishop alerted him to Catherine's premarital indiscretions and extramarital infidelities. A letter of November 12, 1541 from the Privy Council to Sir William Paget, then resident ambassador in France, describes how Henry, on discussing the matter with them, was speechless with shock and emotion before releasing "plenty of tears."[6] For her betrayal, Catherine was rewarded with a trip down the Thames, passing under the tarred heads of her lovers on London Bridge to a temporary stay in the Tower, before, on February 13, 1542, she followed them to the block.

Ever the optimist, Henry married again fifteen months later. This time his bride wasn't an inconstant and giddy girl, but a mature, intelligent, and graceful woman of thirty-three. According to his later lord chancellor, Sir Thomas Wriothesley, Henry never had "a wife more agreeable to his heart" than Kateryn Parr.[7] Certainly, the twice-widowed Kateryn brought experience and wisdom to her queenship, and she relished the opportunity to patronize musicians, artists, playwrights, and churchmen, as well as producing her own scholarship: Kateryn was both the first Queen of England to publish her own book and the first English woman to publish a work of prose under her own name in the sixteenth century. Although she had never had children herself, she had been a stepmother already and knew how to provide maternal care for the motherless young Edward and Elizabeth, and even to their older sibling, Mary. Kateryn was an attractive, steady, and level-headed choice for Henry's latter years.

It is unlikely that he had a similar appeal to her. Before his eye had alighted on her—when she was serving as one of Lady Mary's maids of honor—she had been minded to marry the king's brother-in-law, the handsome Sir Thomas Seymour, and indeed the pair finally wed very soon after Henry VIII's death. But back in 1543, although her husband may have been a king who remained a powerful and decisive force in the governance of the realm, there was no disguising that Henry was becoming aged and grossly fat. The emotional devastations of his life, and the ongoing physical debilitation of his injury, were taking their toll. In 1540, Henry had been given a beautifully illustrated Psalter; at some point in the following years, beside Psalm 37.25, which reads "I have been young and now am old," Henry inscribed in the margin "*dolens dictum*," "a grievous saying."[8]

Over the next couple of years, Henry VIII's decision to go to war with both Scotland and France, and especially his insistence on leading troops against the French himself, can be understood to be as much acts of defying age as driven by foreign policy. Henry had last sought military glory in France in his early twenties; in other words, it was thirty-one years since he had sported armor in the field—armor that needed now to be enlarged quite dramatically.[9] The war against France had as its ambitious aim the taking of Paris in alliance with Emperor Charles V. Henry directed the campaign first against Boulogne, besieging the town and forcing a surrender, so that he could ride through its gates on September 18, 1544 as a conquering hero, Henry V reborn, before returning in triumph to England and leaving his generals in the field to continue the fight.

It was a glorious moment for Henry's ego. Yet, his true sense of his own mortality can be charted by the fact that before his French adventure, and unlike in 1513, he drew up a will—this version does not appear to have survived—and had a new Act of Succession passed by Parliament, which confirmed the legal status of that will. The preamble to the Act states that the grounds for its creation were the king's intentions to "make a voyage royal in his Majesty's most royal Person into the Realm of France, against his ancient enemy the French king," which had caused him "prudently and wisely" to "consider . . . and call . . . to his remembrance how this realm standeth at the present time in the case of succession."[10] He might have been playing the part of an immortal warrior, but he could nonetheless spy death on the horizon. In his absence from England, he appointed Queen Kateryn to rule as regent-general, and he nominated a small regency council to provide counsel for her.

The religious state of the realm also continued to vex Henry. In 1543, Parliament passed the Act for the Advancement of True Religion, which was primarily a proclamation against heretical books, but which also restricted the reading of the English Bible to nobility, gentry, and merchants, barring it specifically from all "women, artificers, apprenticers,

Cum ceciderit non collidetur : quia dominus supponit manum suam.

Iunior fui etenim senui/& non vidi iustum derelictum: nec semen eius querens panem.

Tota die miseretur & comodat: & semen illius in benedictione erit

Declina a malo, & fac bonum: & inhabita in seculum seculi.

Quia dominus amat iudicium: & nō derelinquet sanctos suos: in eternum conseruabuntur.

Iniusti punientur: & semen impiorū peribit. Iusti autem hereditabunt terrā & inhabitabūt in sclm sclī super eam.

Os iusti meditabitur sapientiam: & lingua eius loquetur iudicium.

The page from Henry VIII's Psalter (1540–1), in which, next to Psalm 37.25—"I have been young and now am old"—is the marginal inscription in Henry's handwriting: *dolens dictum*—"a grievous saying." © *The British Library Board, Royal 2 A XVI f45r.*

journeymen, servingmen under the influence of yeomen, husbandmen and labourers"—in short, everyone of a lowly social standing. This was only five years after the command that a Bible in English should be placed in every parish church in the land.[11]

Henry made the reason for this apparent *volte-face* in policy clear in an unusual and heartfelt speech to Parliament at Christmas 1545, a speech so moving that Sir William Petre (pronounced "Peter"), one of his new privy secretaries, wrote to Paget that to hear Henry speak thus was "such a joy and marvellous comfort as I reckon this day of the happiest of my life." It grieved him, Henry said, that "that most precious jewel, the word of God, is disputed, rhymed, sung and jangled in every alehouse and tavern." He had hoped that reading the Bible in English would promote obedience; instead it had produced irreverence and dissension. He bemoaned the religious divisions that had sprung up in the country, complaining about those "too stiff in their old mumpsimus"—too unwilling to change from the mumbled repetition of Roman Catholic practices—and others "too busy and curious in their new sumpsimus"—too quick to embrace the novelties of Reformed thought emerging from the Continent. Henry reduced himself to tears, pleading for unity and charity among his subjects. Few listening, according to Petre, could avoid weeping too.[12]

Cry they might have done, but few were really ready to follow his exhortations. The last year of Henry's life was to be marked by discord that came close to the throne.

3

The Last Year

What would turn out to be the last year of Henry VIII's life was a fascinating, tumultuous period of conflict and contention, as those around the throne jostled for power. The ultimate goal was control of the government after the aging king died. The trouble was, of course, that no one knew quite when that would happen. With the benefit of hindsight, however, we have the privilege of knowing precisely when death would come to call on Henry VIII, and so can see exactly how the events of this last year are pivotal to understanding the context in which Henry drew up his last will and testament, in December 1546.

Much of the storm that would break as Henry drew up his will started to brew earlier in the year. One catalyst was the English defeat by the French at the Battle of St. Etienne in January 1546, for which responsibility lay with Henry Howard, Earl of Surrey.

Surrey had been born into the one of the most important and powerful noble families in Tudor England.[1] He was the eldest son of Thomas Howard, Duke of Norfolk, while on his mother's side he was descended from the dukes of Buckingham, and two of his cousins (Anne Boleyn and Catherine Howard) had been Henry VIII's queens. Probably born in 1517, and named after his king, Surrey had grown up with Henry VIII's illegitimate son at Windsor Castle and at the court of the French king, Francis I, in 1533; in short, he had been reared as a prince. He had also been made a Knight of the Garter at the age of twenty-four. He was a poet of extraordinary power, who invented new verse forms in English, both blank verse and the "Shakespearean" sonnet. He was, though, vainglorious, reckless, and conceited. For April 1543, the *Acts of the Privy Council* include the note that the Earl of Surrey and a small gang had been sent to Fleet Prison for eating meat in Lent and in "a lewd and unseemly manner . . . walking in the night about the streets and breaking with stonebows of certain windows."[2] The historian W. K. Jordan described him very aptly as an "infinitely gifted juvenile delinquent."[3] Nevertheless, his nighttime exploits had not prevented the recognition of his talent, which is why, at the age of just twenty-eight, in August 1545, Surrey had been made Henry VIII's commander-in-chief of the armed forces in France.

Yet, whether from lack of judgment or sheer misfortune, in January 1546 this youthful leader met disaster. At St. Etienne, under his command, the defeated English suffered casualties of between two hundred and one thousand men, and there was no doubting that many of those slain were the highest-ranking military personnel and the cream of English society.

One commentator, the Welsh soldier Elis Gruffydd, blamed the thrashing on Surrey's pride and arrogance. What is not in doubt is Surrey's disgrace. When defeat looked unavoidable, he fled the field of battle, and in his letter to the king blamed the failure not on the leaders but on "a humour that sometime reigneth in English men."[4] It is no wonder that he was soon stripped of his position and recalled home.

In Surrey's place was put Edward Seymour, Earl of Hertford, who had recently known great military success in Scotland. This substitution bred resentment in the thwarted, arrogant Surrey. According to the seventeenth-century historian Gilbert Burnet, at Hertford's advancement Surrey "let fall some words of high resentment and bitter contempt, which not long after wrought his ruin"; another seventeenth-century writer, Lord Herbert of Cherbury, mused that Surrey's behavior "did so little satisfy the king (who loved no noise but of victory) that he ever after disaffected him; for which cause also he was shortly removed."[5] They were right: here Surrey sowed the seeds of his destruction, above all by disappointing his king. Henry would brook no failure. The Battle of St. Etienne would claim its final victim in the vital last weeks of Henry VIII's reign.

Meanwhile, Hertford's appointment in Surrey's place as Lieutenant-General in France removed the former from the center of power for a crucial season over the spring and summer of 1546. Hertford, aged in his mid-forties, was the king's brother-in-law by virtue of being the older brother of Jane Seymour. He was a member of Henry's Privy Council and a brilliant soldier. He was also a man who had a profound sense of his own self-importance, and whose audacity could look like arrogance and pride to his enemies. Reading Hertford's letters, one is struck by his "bold and rude writing": Hertford's handwriting and spelling were rather rudimentary, but "bold and rude" also sums up his peculiar combination of gumption and ill-temper.[6] Imperial Ambassador François Van der Delft thought him "a dry, sour, opinionated man."[7]

The Catholic Van der Delft had good reason, anyway, to dislike Hertford. Although Hertford kept his cards close to his chest, it is evident that he was an "evangelical"—a proto-Protestant. Evangelicals believed in justification by faith alone (as Luther did)—that salvation could be achieved simply through believing in God's grace and the sufficiency of Christ's death on the Cross to wipe away sin. They also held that ultimate authority lay with the Bible, and that the Church needed to be reformed in line with the Scriptures, including by the elimination of images in worship (which evangelicals considered idolatrous) and the removal of practices such as the veneration of saints and pilgrimages to honor relics. Many at Henry VIII's court were opposed to such beliefs.

Hertford's absence seems to have emboldened those of another religious complexion to attempt to seize control of the court in mid-1546. These were the "conservatives," who inclined toward retaining many of the beliefs and practices of the Catholic Church despite having ditched the pope. The key conservative and the chief instigator of a series of high-profile attacks on suspected heretics in the summer of 1546 was Henry's lord chancellor, Sir Thomas Wriothesley.

Wriothesley (pronounced "Rye-zlee") was forty-one years old in 1546 and had been lord chancellor for two years. Born into a family of heralds, he had originally been Thomas Cromwell's man, profiting—as so many of the gentry and nobility had done—from the dissolution of the monasteries.[8] When Cromwell fell, however, Wriothesley continued his own ascent, and in 1540 he had been made one of the king's principal secretaries, before being promoted to the highest office in the land: that of lord chancellor.

Sir Thomas Wriothesley was both astute and dogged. His contemporary, Richard Morison, noted that he was "an earnest follower of whatsoever he took in hand, and did very seldom miss where either wit or travail were able to bring his purpose to pass."[9] Or perhaps George Blage, who had his own reasons to judge Wriothesley harshly, was more accurate when he declared that Wriothesley had "crept full high" only "by false deceit, by craft and subtle ways."[10] The judgment of recent historians has inclined more to the latter view. Professor Peter Marshall concluded that "broken loyalties and betrayals were the stepping-stones of Wriothesley's career."[11] The events of 1546 would suggest that he was—though zealous, hardworking, and possessed of Henry's trust—rather nasty.

Wriothesley's first victim in 1546 was a young gentlewoman from Lincolnshire called Anne Askewe.[12] She had first been arrested in 1545, but then released; yet on May 24, 1546 she was summoned before the Privy Council at Greenwich to be examined on her beliefs about the nature of the sacrament of the Mass. According to her own account, the Councillors urged her to "confess the sacrament to be flesh, blood and bone," but she held that "the bread is but a remembrance of his [Christ's] death, or a sacrament of thanksgiving for it." "As for that you call your God," she declared, it "is but a piece of bread." Displaying deft knowledge of Scripture, she backed up her conclusion by quoting from the Book of Daniel that "God will be in nothing that is made with the hands of men," and that Christ did not literally mean the bread was his body, just as he did not mean he was an actual door, a vine, or a lamb, in his other metaphors quoted in John and 1 Corinthians.[13] Scriptural she may have been, but the beliefs she was expressing were sacramentarian and, in Henrician England, held to be heretical.

Askewe was prosecuted for heresy on June 28, and the next day she was sent to the Tower of London, to be examined by Wriothesley and Sir Richard Rich, formerly Chancellor of the Court of Augmentations. Born in around 1496, the dastardly named Sir Richard Rich was a member of Middle Temple and a lawyer by training. He was also an obnoxious, amoral, and ruthless opportunist who climbed high on the bodies of those more principled than himself. His career, including such positions as Commissioner of the Peace, Attorney-General for Wales, and Solicitor-General for England, should have made him a great devotee of the law; but it was on his perjury that Sir Thomas More and Bishop John Fisher, who both opposed Henry's supremacy over the Church, had gone to their deaths, and, while he owed everything to Cromwell, he had given evidence, too, at Cromwell's attainder for treason. Wriothesley's profit from the monastic suppression was negligible compared to Rich's haul: he filled his pockets as Chancellor of the Court of Augmentations; only the king had benefited more.

In the Tower, Wriothesley and Rich asked Anne Askewe whether she could name any others belonging to her "sect," specifically questioning her about several women: Catherine Willoughby, the dowager Duchess of Suffolk, who was known for her evangelical views; Anne Calthorpe, Countess of Sussex; Anne Stanhope, Countess of Hertford; Joan Champernowne, the wife of Sir Anthony Denny; and Mabel Clifford, the widow of Sir William Fitzwilliam.[14] These queries touched close to the heart of the court: Catherine Willoughby, fourth wife to the late Charles Brandon, Duke of Suffolk, was a close friend of Kateryn Parr; Denny was a

Gentleman of the King's Privy Chamber and a close friend of Henry; and the Countess of Hertford was, of course, wife of the king's brother-in-law who was conveniently in France. It looks like Wriothesley and Rich were trying to condemn Hertford's wife in his absence. The other women in the list were ladies of Kateryn Parr's court.[15]

To persuade her to talk, Askewe was racked, first by Sir Anthony Knevet, the Lieutenant of the Tower, and then, when he refused to proceed further, by Rich and Wriothesley themselves, in an act of savage criminality.[16] "Throwing off their gowns, [they] would needs play the tormentors themselves," racking her till they "almost tore her body asunder," till "the strings of her arms and eyes were perished," till, said Askewe, "I was nigh dead."[17] This was all strictly illegal and highly irregular: torture was rare in cases of heresy and was against the law when done without a permit from the Privy Council, in the case of someone already condemned, or when that someone was a woman.[18] All these criteria applied to Anne. Nevertheless, she refused to indict anyone, even holding out when the racking was done and Wriothesley forced her to sit her broken body for "two long hours reasoning with my lord chancellor upon the bare floor," promising her that should she change her mind, she would want for nothing.[19] When she went to Smithfield for her execution on July 16, 1546, she had to be carried in a chair, because the racking had damaged her so badly that she could not walk. There, before she was burned with two other martyrs, Wriothesley gave her one last opportunity to recant.

What drove such a desperate and determined pursuit of heresy, and why was Askewe so pressed to incriminate others? Historians have suggested that with evangelicals like the Earl of Hertford out of the way, the conservatives, with Wriothesley at their helm, became intent on rooting out heresy, for both sincerely religious but also more earthly political purposes. Had Askewe's spirit been broken as effectively as her body had been, and had she implicated others, she might well have named a number of leading evangelicals at court; and with the evangelicals out in the cold, the conservatives would have ruled the roost.

A scene illustrating "The order and maner of the burning of Anne Askew," included in John Foxe's *Acts and Monuments* (also known as *Foxe's Book of Martyrs*). The contemporary woodcut shows the Lincolnshire gentlewoman Anne Askewe (1521–46) being burnt at the stake, with others, at London's Smithfield on July 16, 1546, having been condemned for heresy and tortured in the Tower of London. *Culture Club/Getty Images.*

There is also evidence that the attack on Askewe was just one part of a calculated campaign. Between Askewe's racking and her burning, Wriothesley moved against someone much closer to the heart of the court, George Blage.

Blage was a courtier—a member of the king's Privy Chamber, a soldier, diplomat, Member of Parliament, evangelical, friend to the poets Sir Thomas Wyatt and the Earl of Surrey, and a poet himself, albeit an indifferent one. He was a close enough companion of the king to have earned the honor of a derogatory nickname—Henry called him "my pig"—and yet, boldly in July 1546, Wriothesley directly targeted Blage.

The evidence used against him was that in May Blage had been heard to mock the Mass by posing the question of what to do if the bread of the Mass were eaten by a mouse, to which he had concluded "that in his opinion it were well done that the mouse were taken and put in the pix"— the pix being the receptacle containing the consecrated bread, to be held up for adoration.[20] These were heretical, sacramentarian beliefs, and on this evidence Wriothesley had Blage arrested on July 11 and, within twenty-four hours, convicted by a jury and condemned to death by fire.

It was an extraordinary miscalculation on Wriothesley's part. Henry was indeed fundamentally opposed to any doctrine that denied the real presence of Christ in the bread and the wine. In 1538, dressed in the white of theological purity, the king had presided in person over the trial of a sacramentarian heretic, John Lambert, at Hampton Court, and Lambert had perished in the flames. The only other person of any standing who espoused these beliefs and escaped the fire in the summer of 1546 was the former bishop, Nicholas Shaxton, who formally recanted.[21] Such evidence suggests, therefore, how fond and furious Henry must have been to intervene to save Blage: the fondness for Blage was coupled with fury at the lord chancellor attempting to reach into the king's own Privy Chamber and pluck out from it a man whom Henry considered to be a good friend as well as a personal servant. As soon as the news of Blage's arrest made it to him, Henry instantly commanded Wriothesley to draw up a pardon; he would not see his pig roasted.[22] The incident reveals the audacity of conservative machinations at court, but also, importantly, the limits on any attempt to force Henry to do anything. The story of the creation of Henry VIII's last will cannot be understood without remembering this characteristic intransigence of the king.

This episode makes the other target of the conservatives—an attempt at an even greater prize than Blage—more incredible. At some point over these months, they tried to indict the queen, Kateryn Parr, for heresy.[23]

John Foxe tells us that Kateryn, an evangelical, was much given to reading and studying the Bible with the ladies of her privy chamber.[24] Furthermore, she took to debating religion with the king, very frankly, and urging him to further reformation of the Church. This he bore well, and even, for a time, seemed to enjoy. But on one occasion perhaps, Foxe suggests, sickly and pained by his leg, Henry grumbled at Kateryn's temerity after she had left, muttering sarcastically: "a good hearing it is, when women become such clerks; and a thing much to my comfort, to come in mine old days to be taught by my wife."

Henry was overheard by Stephen Gardiner, Bishop of Winchester. A trained lawyer, former ambassador, and brilliant but self-important, stubborn, and argumentative cleric, Gardiner opposed Kateryn's religious views, and the opportunity seemed too good to miss. Gardiner soothed the king with the kind of ostensibly reassuring phrases that in reality alarm and disconcert. He had soon "whetted the king both to anger and displeasure towards the queen."[25] Stirred to distrust, Henry allowed Kateryn to be investigated: her rooms were searched for forbidden books, her ladies were questioned, and articles against her were drawn up. It looked as if the queen's life might be on the line.

Given Henry VIII's record, we might be astonished that the famous six-wives ditty ends as it does: "Divorced, beheaded, died/Divorced, beheaded, survived." Kateryn's survival seems to have been wrought by the compassion of one or two individuals who tipped her off, and by her own quick thinking. Foxe tells us one rather improbable story about the damning articles falling from the pockets of one of Henry's councillors, and their being found by "some godly person" and taken to the queen. More convincingly, he also relates that Henry recounted the affair to one of his physicians—either Dr. Thomas Wendy or Dr. George Owen, though Foxe thinks the former more likely—who warned the queen of her precarious position.[26]

Either way, Kateryn was in the know and the next night, when she visited the king, the conversation turned to religion. When Henry sought her opinion, she delivered a speech of submission so artful and persuasive that it is rivaled only by Katherina's morally troubling speech in the final act of Shakespeare's *The Taming of the Shrew* for totality of capitulation.[27] Kateryn spoke of a woman's entire inferiority and subjection to man, who was her head, by whom she was to be governed, commanded, and directed, and questioned how her "only anchor, supreme head and governor here in earth, next unto God" could seek the judgment of "a silly poor woman."[28] "Not so . . . you are become a doctor, Kate to instruct us," Henry retorted, to which Kateryn explained that she had only ever been bold with him to "minister talk," to distract his mind from the pain of his injury, and to profit from the king's learning, and that, in truth, she believed it "very unseemly, and preposterous" for a woman to purport to instruct her "lord and husband." As often with Foxe, we do not know if these words are an invented speech or based on an eyewitness report; but whatever she said was enough to convince Henry. He took her in his arms, called her "sweetheart" and declared that they were perfect friends again.

The next day, as the king and queen, with the queen's ladies, were walking in the gardens, Wriothesley appeared with forty guards intending to arrest Kateryn and her womenfolk. The lord chancellor knelt before Henry and in this deferential pose spoke softly to the king. From a distance, the only words of Henry's heated response that could be heard were "Knave! Arrant knave! Beast! Fool!," and Wriothesley was dismissed from the royal presence.[29] Kateryn had passed her test—or, as Foxe put it, she had "escaped the dangerous snares of her bloody and cruel enemies."[30]

The only surviving account of this whole incident comes from John Foxe, and the lack of contemporary evidence to corroborate it has led some historians to doubt its veracity.[31] Certain details, however, make it seem credible: the fact that it did not appear in Foxe's first edition of 1563 but only later, as if he had learned of it from a witness; his lack of certainty about the identity of the doctor; the words unheard in Henry's dressing-down of Wriothesley; and the fact that Foxe cites his source as being "certain of [Kateryn's] ladies and gentlewomen, being yet alive."[32] What is less plausible is that the mastermind behind the plot was Stephen Gardiner. The bishop was Foxe's "usual suspect," and while Gardiner may have been involved, Wriothesley seems to have played a major role, as he had done in the pursuit of Askewe and Blage.[33] It was he, as lord chancellor, who could have drawn up articles against Kateryn; he who came to carry out the gratifying seizure. Perhaps the initiative also lay, rather, with him.

How can we interpret this series of attacks? In the seventeenth century, Gilbert Burnet was probably right to blame Henry's willingness to have his wife investigated on his growing "distempers" and "peevishness" because of his physical condition.[34] The events also obviously constituted a deliberate and dangerous campaign by the conservatives—and Wriothesley's name is the one that reappears—to undermine and remove the evangelicals at court. Crucially, however, the events also demonstrate that even in his illness, Henry could not be manipulated to do what he did not wish to do. That Henry's stubbornness transcended even his physical deterioration is an important clue to understanding the true nature of his last will and testament. Henry permitted the investigations of Askewe and Queen Kateryn because of his profound commitment to the doctrine of the Real Presence in the Mass, and because of a similarly fervent belief in his position as Supreme Head of the Church, in relation to which Gardiner had persuaded him that his wife had failed him.

The key to Henry's frame of mind is in his response to Kateryn after her deft act of surrender. Once Kateryn had yielded to him, he kissed her and said that "it did him more good at that time to hear those words of her own mouth, than if he had heard present news of a hundred thousand pounds of money fallen unto him." And it no doubt did. Henry saw disagreement with his religious vision as treason. By 1546, he was used to being—indeed, almost expected to be—betrayed, making him hypersensitive to slights and any whiff of treachery. Kateryn's submission probably acted as a real, if temporary, balm to this great wound of betrayal that he bore.

Those who felt the force of the king's ire at their perceived perfidy later in the year would not be granted a similar opportunity to tame the lion.

4

The Final Months

On August 23, 1546, Henry VIII, his councillors and two thousand men on horseback rode out to receive a French party of two hundred gentlemen led by Claude d'Annebaut, the Admiral of France. The visitors were ushered into Hampton Court to ratify the peace that had recently been reached between the two countries. On the next day, the king, dressed in rich apparel, swore to uphold the terms of the peace and signed a treaty with d'Annebaut in the royal chapel, and then the real festivities commenced: a wondrous round of great banquets, elaborate entertainments, and long days of hunting.[1] It was the last great celebration of Henry's reign.

Among those receiving the French Admiral, at Henry's right hand, were Edward Seymour, Earl of Hertford and Lord Great Chamberlain of England, and his fellow warmonger John Dudley, Lord Lisle and High Admiral of England. They had returned to court in early August 1546, having successfully reached a state of Anglo-French amity, and their presence had an immediate impact on domestic politics: they put an end to the fumbled conservative attempts to pluck evangelicals from around the Crown.[2] As the Imperial ambassador mourned in December, "four or five months ago, great enquiries and prosecutions were carried out against the heretics and sacramentarians but they have now ceased, since the Earl of Hertford and the Lord Admiral have resided at court."[3]

Events between the return of Hertford and Lisle and Henry VIII's death would have a direct bearing on the content, conditions, and consequences of the king's will. But what really happened in these last crucial months? The circumstances of the creation of Henry's last will—and its long-lasting ramifications for the reign of Edward VI and beyond—are mysterious. To make sense of the critical, even fatal, slips from power and apparent jostling for position that characterize the ebb tide of the reign, some historians have proposed that the current shifted in favor of the evangelicals at court, and that, with this advantage, they deliberately and murderously conspired through a series of calculated machinations to seize control of the throne after Henry's death.[4]

This conspiracy theory requires that there existed a distinct evangelical faction, deadly opposed to those who sought to limit religious reform, and which had a growing and ultimately decisive influence over the king so that its purported leaders—Hertford, Lisle, and Sir William Paget—could steer him, as the Imperial ambassador feared, "according to their fancy."[5] This view also requires that Henry had deteriorated to such an extent that he could be maneuvred into destroying those he had previously valued, against his better judgment; that he could be manipulated into creating conditions that were favorable to the reformers, and that, in the end, his last will and testament could be altered as he lay dying.

All the accumulated evidence, however, points in a very different direction. The almost inescapable conclusion is that no such elaborate conspiracy theory is needed or justified to explain the events of the last months of Henry VIII's life, and his will was quite literally *his* will: the product of his volition alone.

When Henry VIII revised his will for the last time on December 26, 1546, one of the major changes he made was to remove certain people from among those whom he had previously nominated to make up a regency council to govern the country after his death and during Edward's minority. One of the names he purged was that of Stephen Gardiner. One interpretation therefore is that Gardiner's actions against the queen had turned the king against him, and from that point on the bishop was out of Henry's favor.[6]

This view does not, though, hold up. To begin with, Wriothesley was probably as involved as the bishop. But more than that, Gardiner continued to serve the king after the Parr affair—negotiating with the French ambassador at the end of July, being closely involved in the administration of the realm through his presence on the Privy Council in August and October, and visiting the king at Windsor throughout the autumn.[7] There was no immediate disgrace, for either Gardiner or Wriothesley. In fact, there is evidence of a curious incident at some point over these months indicating that Gardiner was in *more* favor than Lord Lisle. The French ambassador, Odet de Selve, records that Gardiner said something so offensive to Dudley that it made him retaliate with violence, striking the bishop full across the face in a council meeting; Lisle, we are told, was expelled from court for a month.[8] De Selve may have been wrong about his facts: he wasn't present, and the Imperial ambassador noted only that violent words had been exchanged—and did not mention Lisle's expulsion.[9] The event certainly indicates the personal animosity between Gardiner and Lisle; and, if true, it confirms that Henry VIII continued to support his bishop, at least ostensibly, by ordering Lisle's absence.

Indeed, Henry supported Gardiner until his own final months, despite the fact that he had never much liked "wily Winchester."[10] In later testimony (1551) during Edward's reign, when Gardiner was put on trial for refusing to adopt the latest innovations in religion, Henry's erstwhile secretary, Paget, noted that Henry had "misliked the said bishop ever the longer the worse," so much so that Gardiner was "abhorred [by Henry] more than any man in his realm." Paget was convinced that if Henry had lived longer he would have destroyed Gardiner, and he claimed that the king kept a dossier of damning evidence against the bishop, ready to deploy when he needed it.[11] This probably related to allegedly treasonous negotiations between Gardiner and a papal legate when the bishop was an ambassador in Regensburg. Henry VIII may always have suspected, despite Gardiner's protestations, that the bishop remained secretly opposed to Henry's position as Supreme Head and keen to seek a reunification with the Roman Catholic Church.[12]

All this evidence came from those who might be construed as Gardiner's enemies, so one might discount it—except that Gardiner himself inadvertently confirmed something of the same. In June 1547, he told Edward Seymour that the late king used to send him letters "whetting" (scolding) him, "which was not all the most pleasant unto me at the time." Gardiner also related that Henry would often "square" with him, and was once "vehement" with him in the presence of the Earl of Wiltshire, before taking Gardiner aside, comforting him, and explaining that he could "more boldly direct his speech" to him than to someone like Wiltshire.[13] Henry's apparent displeasure, the king reassured Gardiner, was just a sign of their close relationship. The bishop seems to have swallowed this bait hook, line, and sinker, and taken all Henry's future outbursts as evidence of his special favor and invulnerable status, rather than recognizing that Henry found him especially irritating.[14] Yet, despite all this, Henry kept Gardiner close because of his linguistic and diplomatic talent, confident that he could manage him should the bishop act up.

The king's annoyance, however, did reach boiling point at the end of November 1546. Gardiner was invited to "exchange" some lands with the king, but he refused, asking instead to meet Henry to discuss the matter— presumably in the hope of persuading him from the notion, on the basis of his assumed special rapport with Henry. "Exchanging," or more properly giving up, lands to the Crown in return for some form of minimal payment was not an uncommon request: between 1533 and 1547, Archbishop Cranmer surrendered thirty-six manors to the king, the Archbishop of York even more—seventy-four.[15] Gardiner had only ever, grudgingly, lost one. His truculence in response to what was a normal, if tyrannical, demand by the king was therefore enough to anger Henry, who perceived it as disloyalty. The bishop's request to meet the king was stonewalled.

Realizing he had messed up, Gardiner wrote to Henry on December 2, mourning his lack of opportunity to make a humble suit to the king in person, but with a mind so troubled that he was "bold to molest Your Majesty with these my letters." He desired the king to continue to have a good opinion of him, for "I would not willingly offend Your Majesty for no worldly thing. This is my heart, afore God." Above all, he asked pardon if the king had taken badly his "doings or sayings . . . in this matter of lands."[16] Henry's response was an absolutely scorching letter of reprimand, its contained aggression brimming over the finely wrought sentences, which make for excruciating reading. Henry could not "but marvel" at Gardiner's temerity in denying that he had refused to hand over the lands. Henry noted that everyone else, in such matters, had "dealt both more lovingly and more friendly with us" than Gardiner had done. Now, unless Gardiner wished to conform to the Crown's wishes, Henry could see "no cause why you should molest us any further."[17] Gardiner was in the royal doghouse.[18]

Was this a situation created by Gardiner's enemies, "a trumped-up quarrel" where Gardiner was made to look deceitful and thankless through "misleading whispers" in Henry's ear?[19] If so, Sir William Paget would have been the person best positioned to implement any such conspiracy against Gardiner. The masterful Paget had transcended his undistinguished background to climb to the position of principal secretary in 1543. In the intervening three years, he had established himself as the most intimate of Henry's confidants, and he could boast to the Council soon after the king's death that "as it is well known he [the king] used to open his pleasure to me alone in many things."[20] Paget was extremely capable, shrewd, and circumspect, given to wise consideration and wary moderation. Gardiner himself had encapsulated Paget's attitude to religion in writing to him: "you told me once you love no extremities and the mean is best."[21] Gardiner knew this of Paget, because the bishop had been Master of Trinity Hall,

Cambridge, when Paget studied there, and afterward had become both his friend and his patron. It was Gardiner who had introduced Paget into royal service; Paget was, in other words, Gardiner's protégé. In February 1534, he had written to Gardiner: "I esteem myself more bounden to your mastership than to all other."[22]

This is not to say that Paget was slavish in his devotion: in December 1545, Paget wrote to Henry VIII that it was just as well Gardiner was kept "out of the way for a while" as ambassador to France, or else he might try to thwart Henry's policies.[23] He had also earlier expressed concern about Gardiner's severity toward those whom he disliked. But, after cataloguing his mentor's shortcomings, he ended with the indulgent words "God amend all our faults!," recognizing that everyone has defects. We cannot conclude that he had rejected his former patron: to have plotted his downfall would have been an act of great and unanticipated disloyalty.[24] So, while Paget had the means to carry out a conspiracy—as Henry's secretary, writing the words of Henry's peremptory letter, for instance—nothing up to this point makes this plausible. Moreover, Henry's note to Gardiner mentions that the bishop had debated the land-exchange matter with Wriothesley and the new Chancellor of the Court of Augmentations, Sir Edward North, neither of whom would have been involved in any religiously motivated plot.[25] Any notion of Paget trying to bring about Gardiner's downfall through the unreliable business of Gardiner's lands seems highly fanciful.

Instead, as Occam's razor states, the simplest explanation is often the most likely. Gardiner was proud and obstinate, he upset the king, and it was the king who took his revenge: Henry alone decided to remove Gardiner from the list of members of the regency council for Edward's reign, despite all later entreaties to include him. Henry's reasoning? The Imperial ambassador thought it must be to do with Gardiner's religion, but he wasn't an eyewitness.[26] Those who were present heard Henry's explanation directly, even if they remembered his words slightly differently—Gardiner was "too wilful and heady to be about his son," he was "a wilful man and not meet to be about his son," or he was "wilful and contentious, you shall never be quiet, if he be among you." One word was constant: "wilful." Foxe adds that Henry concluded that "he would [en]cumber you all, and you should never rule him, he is of so troublesome a nature . . . Marry . . . I myself could use him and rule him to all manner of purposes, as seemed good unto me, but you shall never do so." Gardiner was stubborn and pig-headed, and not suitable to rule over the young prince.[27] Henry wanted him out. There is no need to look for a plot to explain Gardiner's fall from grace and omission from Henry's last will.

❖

The other obvious name that Henry did not include in the regency council was that of Thomas Howard, Duke of Norfolk. By the time that Henry amended his will to its final iteration, on December 26, 1546, both Norfolk and his son, the Earl of Surrey, had been arrested on charges of treason.

The seventy-three-year-old Norfolk, the most senior member of the powerful Howard family, had been a familiar face at the Tudor court for decades. Astute and experienced, but with a violent temper, the old battle-axe was also obsequious and fawning, ruthlessly obedient, keeping—as Burnet described it—"his post by perpetual submission and flattery."[28] As one of the premier noblemen in the country, he had always longed to be at the heart of power—he was described in 1532 to Charles V as a man who "would suffer anything for the sake of ruling." But he had been obstructed from achieving the ultimate position as preeminent in Henry's estimation by, he believed, Cardinal Wolsey, Thomas Cromwell, and many other imputed enemies.[29] This perpetual sense of resentment was matched, in 1546, by his son's freshly forged rancor, following the debacle at St. Etienne, toward Hertford and other low-born men at court.

Just as with Gardiner, some commentators have construed the dramatic downfall of Surrey and Norfolk as the product of a conspiracy by the supposed evangelical faction of Paget, Hertford, and Lisle in a bid to gain possession of power.[30] It is true that Norfolk himself was convinced, as he wrote to Henry, that "some great enemy of mine hath informed Your

Majesty of some untrue matter against me," while in the Tower Surrey may have been reflecting a similar belief in his injunctions to "Rein those unbridled tongues! break that conjured league!" in his gorgeous and apt paraphrase of Psalm 55, which is all about betrayal by former friends.[31] The Imperial ambassadors Van der Delft and, in early 1547, Eustace Chapuys also considered that the hostility of a reformist faction may have caused the undoing of the House of Howard.[32]

Yet, the actual evidence for this evangelical cabal is remarkably slim. We really have just two main pieces to go on. The first is an enigmatic memo in Wriothesley's files from the end of 1546, which states simply: "Things in common: Paget, Hertford, Admiral [Lisle], Denny."[33] This seems to imply some sort of alliance between them, but it contains nothing of substance on which to build a case. The second, supposedly pivotal, piece of evidence is the assertion by Van der Delft that in the crucial month of December 1546, when the Howards' downfall was secured, "nothing is now done at court without their [Hertford and Lisle's] intervention, and the meetings of the Council are mostly held in the Earl of Hertford's house."[34]

Several historians have followed Van der Delft to his conclusion: that the evangelicals were meeting at the house of their leader, in order to arrogate power.[35] Yet, Van der Delft was wrong. The minutes of the Privy Council clearly state that the councillors did not meet at Hertford's town house, but instead, between December 8, 1546 and January 2, 1547, at Ely Place in Holborn—the town house of Thomas Wriothesley, the arch conservative.[36] Whatever the Council's reason for meeting away from court, it therefore seems unlikely to have been anything to do with a consolidation of reformist power. Perhaps it was simply because Surrey was arrested and detained at Wriothesley's house for five or six days from December 6 or 7, or because, until late December, the king was traveling constantly from house to house.[37] Wriothesley remained at the heart of government—not because he was now suddenly a key player in a reformist faction, but because he simply continued to do his job as lord chancellor. It was business as normal.[38] It is not necessary, and neither is it historically persuasive, to conjure up a conspiracy theory to explain why Surrey and Norfolk were arrested for treason. The reckless, proud Surrey created the circumstances of his own disgrace.[39]

Much mud could be thrown at Surrey. It emerged, for one thing, that he had tried to manipulate the king by encouraging his sister to prostitute herself to him, "as she might the better rule here as others had done." Looking beyond Henry's reign, he had also sought the position of regent for his father—which neatly implicated Norfolk in his treason. Surrey had, too, complained against the dominance at court of men "of vile birth" and the lack of opportunity for the nobility. Above all, he had quartered the royal arms of Edward the Confessor with his own.[40] This last heraldic misdemeanor might not seem terribly significant today, but in a predominantly preliterate age, the visual crime of bearing royal arms was considered a powerful form of lèse-majesté: it was treason, and it comprised the one charge eventually included in Surrey's indictment.[41]

The historian Thomas S. Freeman has written: "Henry Howard's reckless arrogance hit Henry's paranoia like a dentist's drill striking an exposed nerve and provoked the king into a destructive, unthinking rage."[42] Henry's response to Surrey's egotism was his usual reaction to perceived betrayal: revenge, no doubt sharpened, in this instance, by the haste and horror of his sickness. Henry's imprint is over the whole investigation and trial: the list of questions to be asked at Surrey's interrogation was personally edited and amended by Henry himself. And Henry's additions are important: "If a man compassing to govern the king should, for that purpose, advise his daughter, or sister to become his harlot, what it importeth?" reads the original. Henry amended this to: "If a man compassing with himself to govern the realm, do actually go about to rule the king and should, for that purpose, advise his daughter, or sister to become his harlot, thinking thereby to bring it to pass, and so would rule both father and son . . . what it importeth?" reads Henry's version.[43] "Govern," "rule," "rule"—it beats insistently. If Surrey thought he or his father would rule the king and by proxy wear the Crown, they would not be long in having heads to think with.

Rather than evangelical machinations, it was, therefore, sheer arrogant idiocy on Surrey's part that dragged him and his father into the Tudor quicksand. But the revelations had to come from somewhere. The source seems to have been the very opposite of a reformist coup. The disclosure came from Surrey's old friend, and a staunch conservative, Sir Richard Southwell, after some sort of falling out between the pair. This is known because Surrey wrote to the Council seeking to extricate his father from any implication caused by the "stir between Southwell and me."[44] Perhaps Southwell was the "friendly foe" whose betrayal Surrey mourned in the poetry he wrote while imprisoned in the Tower. Indeed, it may be that the main reason Surrey fell out with Southwell was a matter of religion. Surrey seems to demonstrate considerable evangelical zeal in his poetry. Indeed, the similarity between verses by Surrey and those of Anne Askewe are astonishing—one of them was certainly copying the other.[45] This was no evangelical conspiracy against the conservative Howards; by contrast, it is likely to have been a conservative implicating an evangelical friend after a quarrel.

Just as with his grandfather Edward Stafford, Duke of Buckingham (in 1521), and later his son Thomas Howard, 4th Duke of Norfolk (in 1572), Surrey's display of hubristic conceit in an age of personal monarchy and capital punishment was enough to spell his ruin. Pride, treason—and execution—seemed to run in the family. Surrey's foolishness now meant not only his own destruction, but that of his father—yet it is hard to feel sorry for the old man. On the day before Surrey's trial, Norfolk confessed to concealing "high treason . . . most presumptuously committed by my son Henry Howard Earl of Surrey," thereby dictating the judicial outcome for his son.[46] At the trial—a long and public affair on January 13, 1547, which ran from nine in the morning until five at night—Surrey defended himself with wit and courage, but all in vain.[47] In fact, in an age when prosecution and the judiciary were one and the same, and where an indictment could create a crime, the result of Surrey's trial was probably never in doubt: he was found guilty. An Act of Attainder passed through Parliament on January 24 and condemned Surrey and Norfolk to forfeit their lands, chattels, titles, and offices—and lives—to the king.[48] This was a mere rubber stamp to secure the Howard lands. On January 19, 1547, Henry Howard, Earl of Surrey had already been beheaded.

Norfolk, however, was saved by the bell. Destined to be executed on the morning of January 28, another death—the king's—during the night saved his neck. Had his downfall had been the result of a reformist coup, it could be expected that Norfolk would have been quickly dispatched by the new regime, especially during the few days when Henry VIII's death would remain a secret. Instead, Norfolk lived on, left to rot in prison until Mary's reign, when, after his release, the old conniver went on to die peacefully in his bed at the age of eighty. It had been Henry's vengeful will alone that led Surrey and (almost) Norfolk to the scaffold; once his hand had been lifted, there was no further pressure to ensure Norfolk's death.

"The king," wrote Gilbert Burnet, "who never hated nor ruined anybody by halves, resolved to complete the misfortunes of that family."[49] Throughout his life, Henry reacted with vehement vindictiveness toward those who fell short of his expectations. The changes that Henry made to his will to remove Gardiner and Norfolk were a product of his dogged determination, not the effusions of a doddering old man whose course was determined by others.

5

The Making of the Will

I t says something of Henry VIII's character that he retained both his mental acumen and force of will despite his physical condition. For, while he could maintain a grip on his mind, he was fighting a losing battle with his body. In 1546, his perennial attacks of ulcer-induced fever became more frequent. In March, he was febrile for two or three days.[1] Three months later, in early July, when the Askewe affair was playing out, he was noticed to be in a fit of melancholy and sick all night with colic.[2] He was in good health in the late summer, with the French ambassador commenting in September that "the King of England is always in the fields enjoying hunting," but in late October he was indisposed again.[3] In November, he appeared to be gearing up for a new war with the Scots, and Ambassador de Selve thought that a report of the king having a cold was just an excuse to avoid an audience with him as "the fact is that he is as well as usual and goes daily to the fields" to hunt.[4]

By late December, however, soon after he arrived at Whitehall on the 23rd, Henry became seriously ill, enduring an intense thirty-hour onslaught of fever that left him weak and wasted. Van der Delft wrote to the Holy Roman Emperor that "the king is so unwell that, considering his age and corpulence, he may not survive another attack."[5] Henry, too, sensed something terminal in this latest assault, and on the evening of December 26, St. Stephen's Day, he called for a number of his closest councillors, including Paget, Hertford, Lisle, Denny, Sir Anthony Browne and Sir William Herbert—Kateryn Parr's brother-in-law—and told them that he urgently wanted to make some changes to his will.[6]

Denny was dispatched to find the existing testament. Although the first will that we know of had been drawn up in 1544, just before Henry went to war with the French, there may have been two versions of Henry's will prior to this point. For, when Denny returned, Henry dismissed the copy he read out and instructed Denny to look for one "of a later making, written with the hand of the Lord Wriothesley, being secretary."[7] Wriothesley ceased to be secretary in 1543, so this will of "later making" cannot date from any later than that. The 1544 will must have been, then, at least the third version.[8] This may explain why, when Denny returned with a second, apparently later, will, Henry "seemed to marvel that some were left out unnamed in it, whom he said, he meant to have in, and some in, whom he meant to have out."[9] Perhaps even the second time, Denny had returned without the most recent iteration.

Either way, the existing will was not satisfactory and Henry required Paget to draft a new will, and to put "in some that were not named before, and to put out the Bishop of Winchester's name."[10] What Henry was referring to was adding to or subtracting from the list of executors of his will, who were simultaneously charged with forming a regency council on Henry VIII's death to act for his son during his minority, as specified in his Acts of Succession. These were the people in whom, Henry states in the will, "we put our singular trust and confidence," and whom he charged "as they must and shall answer at the Day of Judgement, truly and fully to see this my Last Will performed in all things with as much speed and diligence as they may be" (folios 18 and 16). They were people with extraordinary

An engraving of "Henry VIII, King of England," dated 1548. The Flemish artist was Cornelius Matsys. His depiction of Henry, made soon after the king's death, seems to show the very image of a calculating tyrant. *Hulton Archive / Getty Images.*

responsibility, in whom Henry was investing all his faith for a smooth transfer of power and the efficient functioning of his son's regime.

Henry named the following recipients of his confidence to be his executors and Edward VI's councillors. Ten of them were already members of his existing Privy Council:

> THOMAS CRANMER, *Archbishop of Canterbury*
>
> THOMAS WRIOTHESLEY, *Lord Chancellor of England*
>
> WILLIAM PAULET, LORD ST. JOHN, *Great Master of the King's Household and Lord President of the Privy Council*
>
> JOHN, LORD RUSSELL, *the Lord Privy Seal*
>
> EDWARD SEYMOUR, EARL OF HERTFORD, *Great Chamberlain of England*
>
> JOHN DUDLEY, VISCOUNT LISLE, *High Admiral of England*
>
> CUTHBERT TUNSTAL, *Bishop of Durham*
>
> SIR ANTHONY BROWNE, *Master of the King's Horse*
>
> SIR WILLIAM PAGET, *"our Chief Secretary"*
>
> DR. NICHOLAS WOTTON, *Dean of Canterbury and York*

There were few surprises here. In addition to the usual suspects of Wriothesley, Hertford, Lisle, and Paget, Cranmer had been one of the king's closest confederates since he had found the grounds for, and declared, the annulment of Henry's marriage to Katherine of Aragon. Tunstal, born in 1474, was a scholar and statesman of long standing, a religiously conservative man of moderation and sound judgment who had been a close friend of Thomas More and had served the king as a diplomat, judge, Privy Councillor, and bishop.[11] Lord St. John, too, had had a long political career, serving the king in numerous roles, including as Master of the Court of Wards, Lord Chamberlain of the Household and Lord President of the Privy Council. Despite often having to do Henry's dirty work—telling Katherine of Aragon that her marriage had broken down, acting as a judge at the trial of Bishop John Fisher and Thomas More, and leading royal troops against the rebel Pilgrims of Grace—he did it with grace and

Henry VIII, painted *c.*1537 by Hans Holbein the Younger. *Thyssen-Bornemisza Collection/Bridgeman Images.*

The family of Henry VIII, painted by an unknown artist. This picture, from 1545, depicts Henry VIII at Whitehall Palace with his offspring: his daughters twenty-nine-year-old Mary (*left*) and twelve-year-old Elizabeth (*right*), and, close at hand, his eight-year-old son, Edward, around whom Henry has an arm. It is an idealized image: the wife on Henry's left was not his wife in 1545—Kateryn Parr—but rather his third wife, Jane Seymour, who gave him his son and heir. Curator Brett Dolman has observed that Henry, Jane, and Edward appear very much as a Holy Family, adored by the two princesses. The man in the archway is Will Somer, the king's fool. *Royal Collection Trust © Her Majesty Queen Elizabeth II, 2015/Bridgeman Images.*

The Whitehall Mural, in a 1667 copy by Remigius van Leemput. This arrangement of Henry VIII, Jane Seymour, and Henry's parents—Henry VII and Elizabeth of York—appeared originally, in 1537, as a 9-foot by 12-foot (2.8 × 3.6 meter) mural by Hans Holbein the Younger, at Whitehall Palace. Whitehall burned down in 1698, but two small copies of the mural, including this one, had been made. In the depiction, the closed body language of Henry's parents and wife contrast with his confident, open stance, and Henry's huge masculine shoulders are exaggerated by his voluminous gown. *Royal Collection Trust © Her Majesty Queen Elizabeth II, 2015/Bridgeman Images.*

Henry VIII and the Barber Surgeons, painted in 1540. Here, an old, jowly Henry, in full regalia, is seen giving a charter to the Worshipful Company of Barber Surgeons, whose members are named. On the right can be seen Edmund Harman and John Ailef, two of the witnesses to, and beneficiaries of, Henry's will. *Barber-Surgeons' Hall, London, UK/© Courtesy of the Worshipful Company of Barbers/Bridgeman Images.*

Thomas Cranmer, in a portrait by Gerlach Flicke, dated to 1545–6. Henry VIII's Archbishop of Canterbury from 1533, Cranmer (1489–1556) annulled the king's marriage to Anne Boleyn in 1533, helped create the new Church of England, and ultimately was the man holding the king's hand when Henry VIII died. He was named as a regency councillor and executor in Henry VIII's last will, and went on to be the architect of the Protestant reformation during Edward VI's reign. He was martyred by Mary I. *Universal History Archive/Getty Images.*

The frontispiece of the Great Bible, issued in 1538 and intended to be placed in each parish church in the country. In the illustration, Henry VIII, looming large beneath a rather squashed God, munificently hands the Word of God (*Verbum Dei*) to Archbishop Cranmer (*left*) and Thomas Cromwell (*right*), to be in turn diffused down the social and ecclesiastical ranks. The populace shout "Vivat Rex!" or the vernacular "Long Live the King!," depending on their social status. *Universal History Archive/Getty Images.*

Henry Howard, Earl of Surrey, in a portrait from 1546, attributed to William Scrots. Born in 1517, Surrey was the son of Thomas Howard, Duke of Norfolk. He is shown here wearing an ostentatious doublet and hose, necklace, and garter. The portrait allegorically depicts Surrey's royal descent from Edward the Confessor and Edward III (implied in his unwise heraldic quartering of the royal arms of Edward the Confessor with his own). Surrey was commander-in-chief of Henry VIII's forces in France until 1546, but he was executed for high treason on January 19, 1547. © *National Portrait Gallery, London, UK.*

kindness; Anne Boleyn described him as "a very gentleman."[12] Sir Anthony Browne had been made Esquire of the Body of Henry VIII in 1524, had been sent to accompany Anne of Cleves to England, and had been at Henry VIII's side at the siege of Boulogne. Meanwhile, the elderly, serious, and prudent Lord Russell, with his strong features, battle-injured right eye, and full white beard, came from a dynasty of courtiers. His grandfather had served Edward IV and Henry VII, and Lord Russell had been appointed to the prestigious office of Lord Privy Seal in 1542.[13] Finally, Dr. Wotton was a theologian and career diplomat, and in 1546 was Henry's ambassador resident at the French court. To a man, these were the king's most senior, enduring, and trusted servants.

In addition to these ten, another six men who were not already Privy Councillors were appointed by Henry to Edward's regency council:

> SIR ANTHONY DENNY, *one of the Chief Gentlemen of the King's Privy Chamber*
> SIR WILLIAM HERBERT, *also one of the Chief Gentlemen of the King's Privy Chamber*
> SIR EDWARD NORTH, *Chancellor of the Court of Augmentations*
> SIR EDWARD MONTAGU, *Lord Chief Justice of the Commons Pleas*
> SIR THOMAS BROMLEY, *a puisne justice of the King's Bench*
> SIR EDWARD WOTTON, *Treasurer at Calais*

Denny, Herbert, and North were all obvious candidates. Of the others, Sir Edward Wotton, brother of Nicholas, was absent from the court in 1546 as Treasurer at Calais. He had gone with Browne to collect Anne of Cleves, was evangelical in belief, and a trusted, but not especially close, courtier. Sir Edward Montagu held one of the leading judicial offices in the land. Sir Thomas Bromley was Henry's most intriguing choice, about whom little is known. Although a justice of the King's Bench, he was not the most senior judge, as his title gives away: *puisne*, meaning "inferior in rank," is pronounced "puny" and is the origin of that word in English. It is unclear why this extraordinary honor fell on Bromley rather than, as would have been more normal, the Lord Chief Justice of the King's Bench, then Sir Richard Lyster.[14] There is no evidence to suggest that Lyster, who would attest to the submission and confession of Norfolk on January 12, 1547, was out of favor, and his exclusion is therefore curious. Little wonder that the epitaph on Bromley's tomb reads: "one of the executors of the king of most famous memory, Henry the Eight."[15]

Henry also named a further dozen men to aid and assist the councillors, and these assistants included nine members of Henry's existing Privy Council—including men like Sir Richard Rich; Henry FitzAlan, Earl of Arundel, Lord Chamberlain of the Household; Sir Thomas Cheney, Treasurer of the Household; William Parr, Earl of Essex, and Kateryn Parr's brother; and Sir William Petre, second principal secretary after Paget (see Appendix II for the full list). To their number were added three non-Privy Councillors, including Hertford's younger brother Sir Thomas Seymour and Sir Richard Southwell.

It was these lists of honored advisers that Henry wanted to fine-tune when he felt himself to be close to death, and it is at this juncture that Henry excluded Gardiner as being too willful to be part of Edward's government. Along with him, Henry overruled the suggestion of Thomas Thirlby, Bishop of Westminster, to the ranks of the assistants, saying of him that "he was schooled" by Gardiner.[16] There was also, apparently, one other name at which Henry "made some stick" but was persuaded to accept as an assistant. Professor Eric Ives has plausibly suggested that this might have been Sir Thomas Seymour.[17] Such coaxing was also attempted on Gardiner's behalf; we can surmise that his exclusion mystified and embarrassed the other councillors. In rereading the new list, Paget tried to argue the case for his old mentor, but the king "would in no wise be entreated." Later, Sir Anthony Browne raised Gardiner's name once more, and Henry responded in anger and with threats: "Have you not yet done . . . to molest me in this matter? If you will not cease to trouble me, by the faith I owe to God, I will surely dispatch thee out of my will also; and therefore let us hear no more of this matter."[18] Gardiner was out on his ear, and Henry wasn't having him back. There were also other sundry changes, alterations, and additions: we know they were made, but not what they were. Changes made, the new will, in its final form, was given to Paget to write up "in a book of paper."[19]

Four days later, Henry VIII's last will and testament—all twenty-eight folios drafted by Paget in gorgeous, clear, secretary-hand calligraphy—was ready to be signed and witnessed.

⌐◇⌐

Henry's final will is dated December 30, 1546. It states: "we have signed it with our hand in our Palace of Westminster the thirty day of December in the year of our Lord a thousand five hundred forty and six" (folio 28), and it bears Henry VIII's signature, "Henry R.," at the top and bottom, together with the signatures of ten witnesses. Many of these witnesses were drawn from the gentlemen and grooms of the Privy Chamber: John Gates (brother-in-law to Sir Anthony Denny), Edmund Harman (also Henry's barber-surgeon), William Saint-Barbe, Henry Nevill, Richard Coke, and David Vincent. Three of the witnesses were royal doctors— George Owen, Thomas Wendy, and Robert Huicke—whose presence testified to the soundness of the king's mind. The last witness, whose signature is the most childish and ill formed, is simply given as "Patrec." The historian Lacey Baldwin Smith identified Patrec as the king's flautist, but another likely candidate is Patrick Raynolde, appointed the king's apothecary a month before.[20] The will was then counter-witnessed and signed by a clerk, aptly named William Clerk (folios 1 and 28).[21]

The statement that the will had been signed with the king's hand was not, technically, true. The king had technically not signed anything with his own hand since September 1545. Instead, a system had been developed to save him from the tedium of inscribing his name on state documents. Three designated royal clerks had been given the authority to impress a facsimile of Henry's signature on each document with a stamp made for the purpose, and then delicately to ink in the indentation that remained.[22] Signature by "dry stamp" was therefore a sort of officially sanctioned forgery, and the clerks involved—Sir Anthony Denny, John Gates, and William Clerk—had to be regularly pardoned for "all treasons concerning the counterfeiting, impression and writing of the king's sign" and reauthorized for the months to come.[23] This system was used to authenticate everything issued in the king's name. Examples in 1546 include a license for a widow called Alice Moore to marry Roland Hunt, a groom of the Privy Chamber; the wardship of two "lunatics," Agnes and John Bury, to Paul Gresham in January; a life grant to the king's laundress, Anne Harris; a warrant to the Great Wardrobe for two gowns and two kirtles for "Jane the Queen's fool" in June; and a licence to a yeoman called John Alen to bait bears in Southwark in December.[24] But the dry stamp was also used for documents of far greater significance—everything from grants, bills, leases and pardons, to letters, licences, commissions and warrants. Around a hundred documents every month had been produced in this fashion since its inception, so by December 1546 something like sixteen hundred state papers had been signed by dry stamp. The condition for its use was that the clerks should record each document signed in this way in a schedule, which the king would endorse each month.

On December 30, 1546, Henry VIII's will received the same treatment as any other official state document: it was signed by dry stamp. According to the schedule of documents where the last will and testament was registered, written by Clerk, it was "signed above in the beginning and beneath in the end and sealed in the signet" in the presence not only of the witnesses named above but also Hertford, Paget, Denny, and Herbert.[25] The will was then, according to Clerk, given into the safekeeping of the Earl of Hertford.

Later in the sixteenth century attempts were made to challenge the authenticity of the will on the grounds that Henry VIII had not signed it himself.[26] This was a mischievous and fallacious claim: if it had had any basis in fact it would have undermined the legality of all the documents produced in the last eighteen months of Henry VIII's reign. But Henry's government had been prepared for such eventualities, and applied a belt-and-suspenders approach to ensuring the legality of all documents produced in this way. Even signed by dry stamp, Henry VIII's will was legal and binding.

The real question revolves around the fact that the dry stamp, by definition, did not require Henry to be present to be applied. This made it open to abuse: it is theoretically possible that the will was not signed on the day stated, but at some later stage. This possibility is exaggerated when one considers that Henry VIII's will, witnessed at the end of December 1546, was not registered in the schedule of documents stamped in December, but in that of January 1547, where it is the penultimate item. Naturally, the hypothesis of a later stamping becomes particularly appealing if one is looking for evidence of a conspiracy, for it creates the possibility that Henry VIII was not the sole author of his own last will and testament. It means that some commentators, such as Sir William Maitland, Lord of Lethington and secretary of state to Mary, Queen of Scots, doubted the date of its stamping; much more recently, some historians have even argued that the will was tampered with or added to after its official witnessing on December 30, 1546.[27]

For these historians, only a later doctoring of the will can explain two clauses they think Henry was unlikely to have written. The first (folio 18) stated: "we will that all such grants and gifts as we have made, given or promised to any, which be not yet perfected . . . as they ought to be . . . and all such recompenses for exchanges, sales or any other thing or things, as ought to have been made by use and be not yet accomplished, shall be perfected." In short, any intended gifts, grants, or payments that Henry had promised, but not fulfilled before death, ought to be honored. The second clause of concern (folio 21) was the one authorizing Henry's chosen councillors to "make, devise and ordain what things so ever they or the more part of them . . . shall during the minority . . . of our said son think meet, necessary or convenient for the benefit, honour and surety" of the realm: a sort of carte-blanche to act as they saw fit. As both clauses gave Henry's executors great latitude to remake the post-Henrician world as they wished, they have been seen as "minimal and subtle forgeries" slyly inserted into the will for that purpose.[28]

What evidence is there for this falsification? David Starkey thinks the ten witnesses may have signed a blank sheet, "for the last lines of the will are written more closely together, as though the signatures were already there."[29] Yet, this is patently untrue. The last lines of the will, just as with all those before them, are spaced out on the page with the great precision and care of an expert calligrapher (see page 201); there are no squeezed characters or cramped lines. Where changes have been made to the text of the will, they are minor: there are a total of five interstitial additions and four redactions (mostly striking-out the words "lawfully begotten" accidentally added after Mary and Elizabeth's names), and their mark on the page is evident. Where space has been left for later additions—in the case of forgotten names—the gap is obvious. Otherwise, the twenty-eight-folio will is clearly complete. It flows from one folio to the next without breaks.[30] The redactions and additions that are present make it very clear that it is a physical impossibility that substantive edits were made to this will after the addition of signatures without it leaving some record on the text itself.

Perhaps, David Starkey declares, the will that was signed was "not the text we have." He also offers "incontrovertible evidence" that the will was altered after the supposed date of its making. This proof of the will's later manipulation—or even rewriting—is, he states, that "Sir Thomas Seymour was listed as a councillor in the will" but was only made a Privy Councillor on January 23, 1547. Thus, the will must have been altered after this date.

The trouble with this argument is that Seymour is not listed as a councillor in the will. The testament only appointed Sir Thomas Seymour to be one of the assistants to the sixteen councillors named to make up Edward's regency council, and his inclusion in this list does not imply that he was already a member of the existing Privy Council. He was, rather, one of the three non-councillors among the assistants—and there were the other six non–Privy Councillors among those nominated as regency councillors. In short, rather than Seymour's inclusion being a pivotal fact in the light of which "no modern court would hesitate to overturn Henry's last will and testament," it is a non-fact: neither incontrovertible, nor evidence.[31] The inclusion of Seymour proves nothing.

In fact, the only real suggestion that the will might have been stamped later than December 30 comes from our first point of inquiry: that it was only entered in the register of documents signed by stamp in January. Was this a simple mistake? Surely not—given that the document in question was of preeminent constitutional significance. It is true that this was not the first time that something signed in one month had been included in the register subsequently: the register of documents for October 1546 includes as item 42, "pardon, the bill signed in September."[32]

However, there is more to it than that. In the register, the king's will is introduced with a flourish, and the first two words of "Your majesties last will and testament" are written in extra-large calligraphy: this is not a mistake that anyone was attempting to hide. In fact, it was probably put there precisely to be noticed. It seems likely, as Professor Eric Ives advocated, that the king's presence at the witnessing and stamping of the will had made its inclusion in a separate register of documents to be endorsed by him seem superfluous; but, in the last days, as his impending death became apparent, it seemed suddenly worrying that not having included the will on a register might undermine its legality and legitimacy. It was, therefore, entered into the January register for the ostentatious purpose of proclaiming its authenticity. Had the will been stamped later than its given date, its inclusion so prominently in the January register would surely have done the precise opposite: it would have cast doubt on its legitimacy. Its inclusion, therefore, on the register of documents for January 1547 does not prove that it was stamped at a later date; rather, it suggests that it was indeed stamped in Henry VIII's presence on December 30, 1546.

❖

It was not implausible that the king might yet rally at the time of making his will. But by early January 1547 he was again brought down by a great fever. The French ambassadors noted in mid-January that Henry had been sick for a fortnight and his ulcer had had to be cauterized—the flesh burnt and singed in the vain hope of controlling the weeping infection.[33] State affairs and plans for a military campaign continued: the bishops Tunstal and Gardiner carried on negotiating with the Scots and the French, and Baron de La Garde, captain of the French fleet, claimed to have seen infantry and cavalry gathering outside London, bound, he thought, for Calais or Boulogne or Scotland.[34] On January 17 the ambassadors met Henry and congratulated him on his recovery, for he seemed to them now fairly well, and the king was sufficiently *compos mentis* to discuss business with Paget as late as January 22. Yet, it was a chimera, a mere temporary remission. For Henry was soon in the throes of his last illness. When dawn broke in England, on January 28, the old king was dead.

The will Henry left behind was precisely as he intended it to be. Those named as members of Edward's regency council—and those omitted—were just as Henry had wanted. It is not necessary to look to theories of a conspiracy to explain how, on January 28, 1547, the evangelicals at court held a strong hand.

6

The Faith of the King

T he way in which the evangelicals at court found themselves so well placed on Henry VIII's death has persuaded some commentators that the king foresaw and intended their ascendancy: that, in actual fact, he wanted the zealous Protestantism that was advanced during Edward VI's reign and pursued under the leadership of Edward Seymour and John Dudley. But what does the will have to say about Henry VIII's faith and his intentions for the new reign?

Although he has gone down in history as the man who destroyed the unity of Christendom simply in order to bed his nubile mistress, the truth is that throughout his life Henry was a pious man, and it is little wonder that his last will is an unmistakable testament to his religiosity. It is also a fascinating snapshot of his precise position on the Geiger counter of religious belief in the sixteenth century, telling us where on the dial between Roman Catholicism and radical Protestantism Henry actually fell in the last month of his life.

Henry's faith had been conventional in his youth. He had gone on pilgrimage to the shrine of Our Lady at Walsingham. In 1521, his book

Assertio Septem Sacramentorum (*The Defence of the Seven Sacraments*) robustly defended the pope against Martin Luther's criticisms. This sixteenth-century bestseller had earned Henry the title *Fidei Defensor*, "Defender of the Faith," and the irony of his proudly continuing to use it after his break with Rome seems never to have occurred to him.

When separation from the Roman Catholic Church became necessary to attain his annulment from Katherine, Henry seems to have adopted his new elevation to the position of Supreme Head of the Church of England with alacrity. He reveled in his right to define the religious beliefs of the kingdom, dictating doctrine by composing the Ten Articles (to Establish Christian Quietness and Unity Among Us . . .)—the first doctrinal statement of the Church of England. The King's Book of 1543 was his own personal reworking of a long theological treatise prepared by his bishops. The orthodoxy that these texts decreed was neither consummately Catholic, nor palpably Protestant.

On the one hand, the new Church of England was reformed. Not only had Henry dispensed with the pope, but he saw himself as a reborn Old Testament prophet, king, and judge—in the mold of David, Josiah, Abraham, or Hezekiah—charged with the task of rescuing England from idolatry. In the words of the King's Book, "finding our people seduced and drawn from the truth by hypocrisy and superstition," he had "travailed to purge and cleanse our realm."[1] This effort meant destroying shrines, including that at Canterbury to the great saint of monarch-defying papal obedience, Thomas Becket. It also brought an end to pilgrimages, to the worship of relics, and to the adoration of saints; and it involved restricting the use of images in worship, including dismantling the statues, paintings, and sculptures of saints on traditional medieval rood screens. Reform also served as a partial justification for the dissolution of all the religious houses in England. Their end reflected a theological shift—the monasteries had chiefly existed to pray for the souls of the dead in purgatory. Prayers for the dead, though praised in the King's Book, were omitted from the new English litany of 1544.

Henry reduced the seven sacraments to the mere three of the Mass, baptism and penance—ironically, just as Luther had done—although marriage was later reinstated. In addition, his government commissioned the production of a Bible in English—the first legal English translation—even if Henry was keen to limit its reading audience to those of sufficient social rank to understand it. The frontispiece of this "Great Bible" of 1539 depicts Henry as he wanted to be seen: magnanimously handing out the Word of God to his grateful people, while the Almighty whispers in his ear.

On the other hand, Henry's Church of England was far from recognizably Protestant. His Ten Articles and King's Book continued to affirm the real presence of Christ in the bread and wine of the Mass and asserted that salvation was only possible by both belief and good works, rejecting the potentially anarchic Lutheran dogma of justification by grace through faith alone.

Yet, in the summer before Henry's death, there had been two incidents that suggested that Henry was perhaps rethinking his Church's precarious, idiosyncratic balance between Catholicism and Protestantism. Curiously, the two events have different stories to tell.

The first was that in late July 1546, for the first time in over a dozen years, an envoy from the pope—an Italian called Gurone Bertano—arrived in England and was granted an audience with the king. Did this mean that Henry was considering a rapprochement with Rome? The meeting seemed promising; but two months later, Bertano was given his marching orders.[2]

The second, contradictory, event occurred only a few weeks later. While entertaining Claude d'Annebaut, the Admiral of France, in August, Henry—casually leaning one arm on the shoulder of his archbishop, Cranmer, and his other on d'Annebaut—remarked that France and England, newly allied, had decided to banish "the Bishop of Rome" (the pope) from France and to change "the Mass in both the realms into a communion."[3] Was he "thoroughly and firmly resolved in that behalf," as Cranmer would contend a few years later, or was it a "typical trick of Henry's, throwing a hand grenade into the assembled company to see what reaction it would provoke?"[4]

In London's National Portrait Gallery, there is a painting by an unknown artist, dating from the 1570s, entitled *King Edward VI and the Pope*. Henry VIII, on his deathbed, is shown pointing to his son, thereby nominating his successor, and is attended by a council that includes Hertford and Lisle. Under Edward's feet, the pope has been felled by a book that declares "The Word of the Lord endureth forever," and in the top right, as if through a window, we can see violent iconoclasts at work, pulling down images against a backdrop of ruin and destruction. The message of this later propaganda is clear: Henry intended the radical Protestantism of Edward VI's reign.

This was also the line taken by John Foxe, and, following Foxe, some historians have argued that Henry was indeed intending further reform in the twilight of his life.[5] Together with his bold remark to d'Annebaut, they point to Henry's choice of executors, and specifically to the exclusion of Norfolk and Gardiner, to suggest that he was deliberately tilting the composition of his son's regency council to leave a body dominated by evangelicals who would advance the cause of Protestantism after his death. In the twentieth century, Professor G. R. Elton added that the tutors appointed by Henry to teach Edward—Dr. Richard Cox and Sir John Cheke—would both come out as vehement Protestants during Edward's reign, and that Henry must therefore have chosen them in full knowledge of the intellectual and spiritual influence they would have exerted on his son. Henry, it is argued, must have been converted at the end of his life, and must have been lining up a Protestant triumph.[6]

Is there anything to suggest that this is true? In practice, there seems to have been little religious motivation in Henry's decision to oust Gardiner and Norfolk, except perhaps Henry's awareness that Gardiner's commitment to the royal supremacy was only skin-deep. The real problem with both Gardiner and Norfolk was character: obstinacy and overweening pride. In addition, in the 1540s, the men appointed to be Edward's tutors, Cox and Cheke, were not known Protestants, but rather classical-inspired scholars—humanists—in the manner of Erasmus.[7] They were chosen because they were leading intellectuals and, if anything, moderate in religion. Cox was, for example, one of two men nominated as "indifferent hearers" in the public religious debate between Bishop Gardiner and the Protestant Robert Barnes in March 1540.[8] They may have later become Protestants, but there is no way that Henry would have known this when he appointed them to instruct his heir, and little should therefore be read into it. Finally, Henry's remark to d'Annebaut and Cranmer seems so outrageous a suggestion—and so completely at odds with happily burning Askewe and others a few months earlier for believing precisely the same thing—that we must surely regard it as a piece of playful and preposterous banter.

Above all, Henry's will itself gives us clues about what Henry believed at the very end of his life. For Henry was an inveterate corrector of theological texts, and if he had spotted any error in the religious pronouncements of his will when it was read to him a month before he died, it is hard to believe that he would not have altered it.

The will's opening words are: "In the name of God and of the glorious and blessed Virgin our Lady Saint Mary and of all the holy company of Heaven" (folio 1).[9] Although Henry did not identify by name ten specific saints as his father had done in his will, nor was he as fulsome in his devotion toward "this most Blessed Mother ever Virgin, our Lady Saint Mary" (as Henry VII's will has it), this is conventional enough and markedly Catholic in style.[10] Later wills of his councillors do not mention the Virgin Mary; even Gardiner, who made his will in the safely Catholic reign of Mary I, on January 28, 1558, committed his soul to "the infinite mercy of Almighty God" and the Virgin Mary did not get a look in—although Gardiner did ask for the "intercession of all the company of Heaven."[11] Henry, in fact, mentions the Virgin Mary and the saints twice: a few pages in, he imperiously states that "we do instantly require and desire the Blessed Virgin Mary his Mother with all the holy company of heaven continually to pray for us" (folio 3). In Henry's world, things are not requested, but demanded, even of the Mother of God.

The second indication of Henry's faith lies in his early confirmation of his supremacy: he is "in earth immediately under God the Supreme Head of the Church of England and Ireland" (folio 1). It is not surprising that such a central plank of Henry's conception of the religious universe is mentioned boldly and upfront. Then he moves on to explain his theology of salvation: how he believes human beings are made right with God.

He states his belief in "original sin"—the conviction that he is, as "all mankind is mortal and born in sin" (folio 1). He affirms his understanding of the divinity: God, who is Almighty, presides over a "transitory and wretched world" and provides "great gifts and benefits." Henry acknowledges his unworthiness to receive these gifts—"our self insufficient in any part to deserve or recompense the same" (folio 1)—but three things, Henry believes, will free him from this wretched state. Chief among God's gifts is the offer of redemption through the person of his son, through whose "most precious body and blood in [the] time of his passion" (folio 3) mankind can be saved and attain eternal life. In addition, Henry notes both the importance of repenting one's "old and detestable life" (folio 3) and, twice, that a person must endeavor "to execute in his lifetime . . . such good deeds and charitable works as scripture demandeth" (folio 1 and similarly on folio 2). The greater his "estate, honour and authority in this world" (folio 2), the greater his good works should be. Salvation, then, comes from Christ's death, the believer's repentance and the performance of good works in life.

Finally, Henry completes his doctrinal statement by stating that he "most humbly and heartily" commends and bequeaths his soul to God, in the hope of everlasting life, but knows that his body, once his soul has departed, will remain "but as a cadaver and so return to the vile matter it was made of . . . for it is but ashes and to ashes it shall again" (folio 4).

This is a thoroughly conservative, theologically orthodox statement of beliefs. Its conception of salvation is far from Lutheran. It is also worth noting what it does not mention. Henry does not call God "Father," as Sir Anthony Denny's testament of 1549 will do; he does not refer to Christ as "Jesus" as the wills of Sir William Parr's (1548), Thomas Wriothesley (1551), and Stephen Gardiner (1558) go on to do, nor does he repeat an oft-used phrase praising "the infinite mercy" of God.[12] Henry's notion of God seems

The first folio of Henry VIII's last will and testament, from the National Archives. Henry's will opens with the king's signature by dry stamp and the words "In the name of God and of the glorious and blessed Virgin our Lady Saint Mary and of all the holy company of Heaven." *The National Archives.*

not to have been personal or familial, nor indulgent, but rather a hierar-
chical figure with whom Henry had a contract. He makes no mention of
the Holy Ghost or God's Trinitarian nature, as Denny and Southampton
both do, and in this, in comparison to other wills of the period, his theology
is closest to Gardiner's.[13] The language of the will leaves us with no sense
of a man about to press further into Protestant reform.

Pressing the tip of his nose to death's doorway also seems to have given
Henry a pragmatic, Pascal's-wager-style approach to the possibility of
purgatory: it might well not exist, but it was less risky to assume it did.
Prayers for the dead might have been omitted from the recent litany, and
monasteries may have been closed—but Henry wanted his soul prayed for,
just in case. He left lands, worth an annual revenue of £600, to the Dean
and Chapter of St. George's Chapel at Windsor Castle, in exchange for
two priests to say daily masses "perpetually while the world shall endure"
(folio 7) and four solemn obits (requiem masses to pray for the soul of a
deceased person) each year.

In order that these prayers might be heard more favorably by the
Almighty, Henry also decreed that alms worth one thousand marks (or
£666 13s 4d) should be given "to the most poor and needy people that may
be found" (folio 6)—although in typical, snooty Henry VIII–style, these
poor and needy people were not to be just any riffraff: "common beggars
as much as may be avoided" (folio 6). In exchange for cash, these poor
people were also required to pray "heartily to God for remission of our
offences and the wealth of our soul." At the quarterly obits, another £10
was to be given to the poor, and, in addition, Henry used his will to found
a body of thirteen "poor knights," who were each to be given twelve pence
every day—a total of £17 16s a year, whilst their head and governor was to
receive an additional £3 6s. 8d. yearly. He charged his executors with fulfilling
these conditions "as they will answer before Almighty God at the dreadful
Day of Judgement" (folios 8–9). In short, some philanthropic impulse notwithstanding, Henry committed the equivalent of £1,327 2s 8d a year to pay
for his soul's progress through purgatory, a sizeable investment that suggests
strongly that Henry had doctrinally not moved far from Catholicism.[14]

In fact, the only religiously unorthodox aspect of Henry's life was the way he left it: that simple squeeze of Cranmer's hand, and not receiving the full rites of extreme unction. Yet, Henry's own Ten Articles of 1536, while deeming confession and absolution by priests to be necessary, had removed extreme unction from the list of sacraments. Henry didn't end his life—just as he hadn't lived it—as a Protestant, but rather in his own special, idiosyncratic religious position: reform coupled with fairly orthodox Catholic theology. This is the position of faith that his will reflects. To the end, Henry did not waver from his course but kept to the doctrine of the English Church that he himself had created—and which he intended his son's rule to maintain.

7

The Succession

There is a very telling line in Henry's will: a sentence that goes to the heart of what he tried to achieve with his life. He states: "our chief labour and study in this world is to establish him [his son, Edward] in the Crown Imperial of this realm after our decease in such sort as may be pleasing to God, and to the wealth of this realm, and to his own honour and quiet" (folio 19). Henry's chief labor in this world had, indeed, been to ensure the smooth transfer of the crown to a son, for the blessing and surety of the realm; it is this mission that explains both Henry's most radical act—breaking with Rome—and his tabloid fame as the husband of six wives. It was also the primary mission of his will.

Having established his religious credentials, made provision for his soul, and outlined plans for his funeral, Henry dedicated the majority of his last will and testament—fully some 3,550 of 6,110 words, or almost 60 per cent—to plans for the succession. This was pragmatic—Henry offers a workable blueprint in the case of all possible eventualities—but it is hard not to detect the emotion behind these many clauses. The prospect of dying when one's children are young is an agonizing worry for every parent. For

Henry, it also meant that he might fail his own father. In the first half of the sixteenth century, everyone accepted that to ensure a peaceful succession, one of the primary responsibilities of a monarch was to produce at least one adult male heir—that is, a boy of at least fifteen years old—and, ideally, a spare, in the case the first should die (as Henry's older brother, Arthur, had done). Henry had not done this, and while he had been on the throne for over thirty-seven years and seen off the last of the Plantagenet threats, the rule of the Tudors was only two generations old and the accession of a minor had potential to plunge the country back into the instability of the Wars of the Roses. Having married and remarried in the hope of sons, Henry anxiously outlined in his will how, with only one boy-child directly in line to the throne, the country was to be ruled after his death, how his "entirely beloved" councillors and executors (folio 22) were to help manage "the sure establishment of the succession" (folio 9), and what to do if Edward died without an heir. This was the will's most urgent and important task.

With the Acts of Succession of 1536 and 1544, which rendered Mary and Elizabeth illegitimate, Henry acquired the statutory right to name his successor in his last will or by letters patent.[1] The Act of 1544 had also, in a belt-and-suspenders approach, laid out a basic line of descent: the crown would go to Prince Edward, and if he were to die without children it would pass to "Lady Mary the King's Highness' daughter" and the heirs of her body; and if she were to die without children, to "Lady Elizabeth the king's second daughter," though even here it reiterated the right of the king to limit this inheritance through any conditions set out in his last will or letters patent.[2] So, the will had crucial legal and constitutional significance for the future of the realm.

The will gives seven stages of succession, each with conditions. The first is the most obvious. It states that:

> . . . *immediately after our departure out of this present life, our said son Edward shall have and enjoy the said Imperial Crown and Realm of England and Ireland, our titles to France, with*

all dignities, honours, and pre-eminences, prerogatives, authori-
ties and jurisdictions, lands and possessions to the same annexed
or belonging to him and his heirs of the body lawfully begotten
(folio 10)

Edward and his lawful, natural children were in direct line to the throne. But what if Edward were to die without such heirs? Although, in their wills, none of his predecessors had thought to make provision for such contingencies, Henry VIII was not content to let the future find its own way.[3] If Edward died without heirs, he specified that the crown was then to pass, secondly, to "the heirs of our body lawfully begotten of the body of our entirely beloved wife Queen Kateryn" (folio 10). Even in the last month of his life, Henry remained hopeful that Kateryn Parr would yet bear him a son, but his optimism went even further. Failing any heirs by Queen Kateryn, he next appointed his heirs from "any other our lawful wife that we shall hereafter marry" (folio 10). You have to hand it to Henry: this six-times-married, fifty-five-year-old man, whose father had died at fifty-two, and whose grandfathers had perished at around twenty-six and forty, still believed—a month before his death—that there was ever the possibility of marrying again and fathering more children.

In the unlikely event of these scenarios not being realized, the crown would then pass to "our said daughter Mary and the heirs of her body lawfully begotten" (folio 11), upon condition that her choice of bridegroom was approved by Edward's Privy Council, in writing. If she died without heirs, the crown was to move on to "our said daughter Elizabeth and to the heirs of her body lawfully begotten" (folio 12), with the same condition about acquiring the approval of the Council to marry. Yet, despite nominating his daughters as his heirs and requiring them to bear lawfully begotten children, they themselves remained in an ambiguous position: still illegitimate. At one point after their names, the words "lawfully begotten" are neatly, but decisively, crossed out (folio 12). Did Henry not foresee the precarious footing on which he put any future rule by his daughters? Did he believe the prospect so unlikely that he did not think to repeal the illegitimacy into which he had cast them, in high dudgeon, in 1536? Probably, Henry's considered opinion was that his marriages to Katherine of Aragon and Anne Boleyn had genuinely been annulled: it was the only belief that freed him from painful cognitive dissonance. But therefore, it proceeded that Mary and Elizabeth were unredeemably bastards.

There is a similar mystery over Henry's sixth succession scenario. If all the above failed—if neither Edward, Kateryn Parr, any future wife, Mary, nor Elizabeth bore heirs—then the crown was to pass to "the heirs of the body of Lady Frances, our niece, eldest daughter to our late sister the French Queen" (folio 13). Lady Frances Grey was the daughter of Henry's younger sister, Mary Tudor (who had indeed been married to Louis XII of France) and Henry's best friend, Charles Brandon, Duke of Suffolk. Frances, in turn, had married Henry Grey, Marquess of Dorset, the grandson of Edward IV's queen, Elizabeth Woodville, and by 1546 had borne him three surviving daughters, the ladies Jane, Katherine, and Mary. For some reason, Henry decided to overlook his living niece, Frances, skipping her generation in favor of her offspring. The reason is unclear. Professor Eric Ives suggested that the issue was either something personal to do with Frances, or it may have been a comment on her husband, as it was assumed at this stage that if a woman became queen, her husband would assume the title of king.[4] This latter seems most plausible as this high-ranking peer is conspicuous by his absence from either the list of sixteen regency councillors or the twelve assistants named in Henry's will. Norfolk and Gardiner were not the only ones being disregarded.

In fact, nominating Lady Frances's heirs meant an even greater omission: it ruled out the descendants of Henry VIII's older sister, Margaret Tudor, whose son James V had been King of Scotland, and whose granddaughter Mary was now Queen of the Scots. By all the normal rules of hereditary and dynastic succession, Mary, Queen of Scots, ought to have had precedence over Lady Jane Grey; but in this instance, Henry exercised his right to determine the succession through his will

The songe of Aus
teyn & Ambrose.
Prayse the
O god we knowlege
the to be the lorde.
All therthe moughte wor
ship the, whiche arte the father
everlasting
To the crie furthe all aun
gelle, the heauens, and all ye
powere therin
To the thue crieth Cheru
byn and Seraphyn contynually.
Forasmuche as you have desired so simple
a reason to writing in so worthye a booke

BOTH PAGES: Illuminated pages from a compilation of prayers belonging to Lady Jane Grey, but derived from various books of devotion and written in Queen Kateryn Parr's own hand. Commonly known as "Lady Jane Grey's Prayer Book," it is almost certainly a deathbed gift from Kateryn to Jane in early September 1548. At that time, she was living in Kateryn Parr's household and became the chief mourner at her funeral. © *The British Library Board, Harley 2342, ff.74v–75.*

very deliberately. It is worth noting just how unusual this was: none of his recent namesakes—Henry V, Henry VI, nor Henry VII, for example—had attempted anything so grandiose as to interfere, in their wills, with the time-honored pattern of male primogeniture in royal succession.[5]

After war with the Scots in the early 1540s—including the humiliating defeat of them at Solway Moss, which arguably hastened the death of James V—the accession of the infant Mary to the Scottish throne had triggered Henry VIII's interest in exercising de facto rule over the whole of the British Isles. To do this, he had attempted to have Mary delivered to England to be brought up and married to Edward. At the Treaty of Greenwich in July 1543, Mary's mother, Marie de Guise, had promised that although Mary would remain in Scotland until she was ten, she would then marry Edward. However, the treaty was almost immediately all but renounced. In retaliation, Henry struck Mary and her descendants from the line of inheritance to the English throne.[6]

Henry had one final provision: if the heirs of Lady Frances did not produce issue, the crown would move to the heirs of Lady Eleanor, second daughter to Henry's sister, Mary Tudor (folio 13). Wife to Henry Clifford, Earl of Cumberland, Eleanor died in 1547, leaving one daughter, Margaret. This Margaret was the last descendant Henry specified in his will. Then, he gave up his meddling with the future. If none of the above were able to produce heirs, Henry ruled that the imperial crown should go "to the next rightful heirs" (folio 14).

❖

All of this, of course, was provision for a seriously worst-case scenario. Henry confidently hoped that his throne would be in the possession of his son Edward, and to help the young king through the potentially tricky years of his inevitable minority Henry also came up with a plan that he hoped would ensure a smooth transition from his reign into a mature, balanced and secure government under Edward VI's headship. This was his plan for a regency council of sixteen wise, trusted, and well-beloved councillors, who would rule England in Edward's stead.

The situation in which the throne was inherited by a minor had occurred several times in English history: Edward VI's was to be the sixth minority kingship in England since 1216. In an age of personal kingship, when a monarch needed to rule as well as reign, a minority was a deeply problematic and unstable time: an invitation to civil war, an incitement to noble tussles over position and precedence, and an opportunity for the unprincipled to seize power.[7] Little wonder that the text often cited was Ecclesiastes 10, verses 16–17: "Woe to thee, O land, whose king is a boy!" It was Henry's hope that a council of sixteen good men and true would steer the young Edward through these precarious years.

In fact, it had been decided even before Edward's birth. Henry and Thomas Cromwell had outlined in the Act of Succession of 1536 that if the king died before a future son reached eighteen, then the governance of the realm should be conducted by his natural mother and "of such other your councillors and nobles of your realm as Your Highness shall limit and appoint by your last will made in writing signed with your most gracious hand."[8] As Edward's mother had died in 1537, only the Council nominated by Henry in his last will held this power.

This reading of Henry VIII's will and intention was challenged in the 1960s by Professor Lacey Baldwin Smith, who argued that we cannot take Henry's plan at face value. Baldwin Smith thought there was no way that Henry seriously intended to legislate for conciliar rule because it was "totally out of tune with prevailing political theory, which was authoritarian to its very core."[9] Either he was "a fool or a senile old man" to propose something so unworkable, or, Baldwin Smith argued, Henry did not intend it as a model of rule but as a kind of Damoclean sword—a means of controlling his courtiers by dangling before them the prospect of whether they would be in or out.[10] This is highly speculative and there is little evidence to support it. In fact, not all of those named regency councillors and executors even knew before the king's death that they had been nominated—Bishop Cuthbert Tunstal, for one, only found out afterward—so it seems unlikely that the composition of the council was used as a weapon of political manipulation.[11]

The weight of history also argued for Henry to adopt a conciliar solution to the problem of his son's minority. After the accessions of the fourteen-year-old Edward III in 1327 and ten-year-old Richard II in 1377, councils had effectively ruled in lieu of the nominal king. For Richard, there had been no official minority—the illusion of the child-king ruling had been maintained, while the Council made all the actual decisions.[12] Richard II's eldest paternal uncle, John of Gaunt, as the most senior royal, played a crucial role in this council—one historian, Gwilym Dodd, has argued that even if he was not technically a regent, in reality he was—but the specified form of government thought appropriate for minority rule was a shared council, from which, at first, John of Gaunt was specifically excluded.[13]

More recent historical precedents—Henry VI, who became king at nine months old in 1422, and Edward V, who acceded in 1483 at the age of twelve—had been of single nominated protectors or regents. In the cases of both kings, this had been their uncles, the dukes of Gloucester. Yet Humphrey, Duke of Gloucester, only had the title of "protector" in 1422—it did not carry with it the right to rule, and it was terminated in 1429 when Henry VI was seven years old. Henry VIII would not have thought it a suitable arrangement for his nine-year-old son. Even more compellingly, the transformation of Richard, Duke of Gloucester, into Richard III through the betrayal and deposition of his nephew, the boy-king Edward V in his care, revealed the perils of minority government under a single head and gave a voluble historical warning of the dangers of handing power to a "protector."

In addition, recent research by Dr. Joanne Paul suggests that Baldwin Smith was wrong to assume that rule by council did not represent contemporary political ideas in the sixteenth century: instead, the idea of a council was being turned to with ever greater frequency. She notes that Thomas Starkey, in his *Dialogue Between Pole and Lupset* (circulating in manuscript in 1529–32), had proposed a specifically English conciliar solution to the question of the highest form of political rule. Moreover, Machiavelli had warned against depending too much on a single counselor, and while we cannot be sure that Henry ever read *The Prince* (published 1532), the ideas contained within it were well known in England by the 1530s and 1540s.[14] A draft bill by Christopher St. Germain, although never passed, had proposed a "great standing council" in 1531, and the King's Privy Council had acquired its new importance and footing in 1540. Abroad too—in Spain and Venice—the large, structured council had become an increasingly important institution of power. In theory and practice, the council as a solution to rule was at the cutting-edge of political thought by the mid–sixteenth century.[15] It was the most practical and sensible scheme that Henry could have concocted. A regency council with the full and unfettered authority of the crown gave Edward's minority the best chance of succeeding.

So that is what Henry intended. But it is not what happened.

8

The Transfer of Power

Henry VIII may have died at around two o'clock on the morning of Saturday January 28, 1547; but for several days, his death was kept a secret.[1] Everything carried on as normal. Parliament, which should instantly have dissolved upon the death of the king, remained in session. Food continued to be conveyed with all the usual ceremony and trumpet fanfare to the king's chambers. Ambassadors were kept in the dark.[2] This was not unusual—Henry VII's death had been concealed in the same way—but it was crucial to the ambitions of two men: it gave Edward Seymour, Earl of Hertford and Sir William Paget a chance to lock down power and to implement a hastily conceived plan.

Although there had been no conspiracy over the contents of Henry's will, and the old king had remained in full, and capricious, control of events until he lay on his deathbed, it seems to have dawned on Hertford and Paget near the very end that if they placed a wager on the hand that fate had dealt them, they had potential to win big. The power of the king—and, especially, the 1534 Act that made it treason to speak of the death of the monarch—meant that Hertford and Paget did not dare to engage in the irrevocable act of plotting their place in a post-Henrician world until they could be convinced that his deterioration was irreversible. Until such time, it was too risky to bet against his sudden recovery—they had seen him rally on many occasions. But at some point in those very last days, they became confident enough to go for broke.

We know this because of a later letter written by Paget to Hertford, from July 1549. This is a vital piece of evidence, because it was a private letter in which Paget had no reason to dissemble.[3] The context was that Paget was writing, in a state of high emotion, to offer advice on how to deal with a rebellion in the West Country. Fearful that this revolt would bring the end of Edward VI's reign and the ruin of Hertford (who by now was Duke of Somerset and preeminent as England's Lord Protector), Paget urged him to remember that he had once promised to follow Paget's advice in all things:

> *Remember what you promised me in the gallery at Westminster, before the breath was out of the body of the King, that dead is. Remember what you promised immediately after, devising with me concerning the place which you now occupy, I trust, in the end to good purpose, howsoever things thwart now. And that was, to follow mine advice in all your proceedings, more than any other man's. Which promise I wish Your Grace had kept. For then I am sure things had not gone altogether as they go now.*[4]

So it is clear that, as the king lay dying, Paget and Hertford had whispered together in the long gallery at Westminster and made promises to each other about what the future would hold. During that night of January 27–28, 1547, immediately after Henry's death, they had begun to plot together to elevate Hertford to "the place which you now occupy": the position he came to assume as Lord Protector of England. There was one condition: that Paget would become his right-hand-man, his chief adviser, to be heeded in all things.[5] This was the deal they struck as Henry VIII gasped his way into the grave, and before his body turned cold.

The two men were in prime position to capitalize on Henry's death: Paget and Hertford were Henry's trusted confidants—his chief secretary and his brother-in-law, his closest of friends. They were also immensely capable and ambitious. On January 29, the former Imperial ambassador, Eustace Chapuys, who was briefly visiting England—and still unaware that Henry was dead—speculated that if the king were to die, "it is probable that these two men will have the management of affairs, because, apart from the king's affection for them, and other reasons, there are no other nobles of a fit age and ability for the task."[6]

Hertford and Paget were thick as thieves. In another letter, from May 1549, Paget told him that he loved him "so deeply in my heart as it cannot be taken out," while in his letter of July 1549 Paget would not only compare their relationship to that between a master and servant, but also to that between spouses: "I have ever desired your authority to be set forth, ever been careful of honour and surety; both for now and for evermore, ever glad to please you, as ever was gentle wife to please her husband, and honest man his master I was."[7]

Finally, they were well placed to seize control on Henry's death because Hertford had possession of the pivotal constitutional document at the time of the transition: Henry's last will and testament.

❖

When Henry breathed his last, Hertford and Paget swung into action with one accord. Speed and boldness were of the essence. Within hours of Henry dying, the earl left with Sir Anthony Browne, Master of the Horse, to secure the person of the new king, Edward, who was at that time at the town of Hertford, some twenty-five miles from Westminster.[8] By the next evening, Sunday January 29th, Hertford had transported the young monarch thirteen miles south to Enfield, where Princess Elizabeth was living. It was at this juncture that Hertford told Edward and his half-sister of their father's death, and, according to Edward VI's first biographer Sir John Hayward, "they both brake forth into such unforced and unfeigned passions . . . never was sorrow more sweetly set forth."[9]

Three letters, two from Hertford himself, give us our only clues as to how the process of assuming power was managed between the time of Henry's death and its public proclamation. The letters demonstrate the way in which Paget and Hertford were carefully controlling the flow of information and managing the unfurling of events. That much business, which no longer survives, was being done—or at least, that Hertford was sleepless and agitated—is also betrayed by his first letter, written between three A.M. and four A.M. on Sunday the 29th, after receiving an urgent note from Paget between one A.M. and two A.M.—just twenty-four hours after Henry's death. The matter so pressing as to prevent sleep was Henry's will.

In Hertford's haste to reach Edward, he had forgotten to give Paget the key to the box in which the will was stored. As the will was the vital document on which their access to power was based, Paget's letter asked for the key and Hertford's thoughts on whether the contents of the will should be made public. Hertford replied that they should consider very carefully how much of it "were necessary to be published for divers respects I think it not convenient to satisfy the world." Hertford suspected it would be sufficient when making Henry's death known for Paget to have the will with him and to be able to name Henry's councillors and executors. They would then deliver its contents in Parliament on Wednesday morning. Before that, Hertford urged, the two of them should meet and agree precisely what the contents purported, so that "there may be no controversy hereafter." They needed to decide a party line. Hertford also enclosed the key. The urgency and gravity of this communiqué was conveyed by the endorsement on its exterior: "To my right loving friend, Sir William Paget, one of the King's Majesties Two Principal Secretaries. Haste, post haste, haste with all diligence, for thy life, for thy life."[10]

Hertford's second letter is dated eleven P.M. on Monday, January 30. He wrote to the Council discussing the possibility of instantly offering a general royal pardon, which they had raised in their letter, and instructed them to wait until Edward's coronation so that the new king would benefit from the praise and thanks of the people.[11] Hertford was already starting to act as though he were in charge. He noted, in the first time this phrase was used of Edward in the surviving papers, that he intended to have "the king's majesty" "a-horseback tomorrow by xi of the clock"—eleven A.M.—so that by three P.M. on January 31 they should be at the Tower of London.[12] He also urged the Council to inform Anne of Cleves of the king's death; we do not know when Henry VIII's widow, Kateryn Parr, learned of the news.[13]

Our final clue as to the handling of those days comes from another letter from 1549, written by a former servant of Sir Anthony Browne. Hertford evidently decided to use the opportunity to persuade his traveling companion, as they arrived at Enfield with Edward, to accept the arrangement that he and Paget had agreed:

> . . . *communing with my Lord's Grace [Browne] in the garden at Enfield, at the King's Majesty's coming from Hertford[,] gave his frank consent [in] communication in discourse of the State, that his Grace should be Protector, thinking it (as indeed it was) both the surest kind of government and most fit for that Commonwealth.*[14]

Hertford now had two members of the Council onside.

On the morning of January 31, Lord Chancellor Wriothesley, in tears, announced the king's death to Parliament and read out the sections of the king's will containing the details of the succession.[15] Later that day, Edward was proclaimed king, and when he and his uncle rode into London, the new monarch was saluted by cannon-fire from ships and from the Tower, where apartments had been lavishly dressed for the young king.[16]

That very afternoon, the regency council, as constituted by the will, gathered for its first meeting, even though three of the sixteen members were not in attendance: Dr. Nicholas Wotton, still resident at the French court; Sir Edward Wotton, who remained in Calais; and Sir Thomas Bromley. The minutes of this meeting noted that Henry's will had given them "full power and authority . . . to do any act or acts whatsoever that may tend to the

EARL OF ESSEX.

TOP: Kateryn Parr as Queen of England, painted *c.*1545 by Master John. Far from the dowdy nursemaid of legend, Kateryn Parr (1512–48)—Henry VIII's sixth and last wife—was an attractive, sartorially adventurous, and graceful woman, who made an intelligent and mature companion for Henry's last years. Her final, and fourth, marriage was to Henry's brother-in-law, Sir Thomas Seymour, in 1547, and she died, following her first childbirth, in September 1548. © *Stapleton Collection/Corbis.* RIGHT: Thomas Cromwell, Earl of Essex. This image of Cromwell (1485–1540), after Hans Holbein the Younger, is an early 17th-century copy of a painting that we can date to c.1532–3, early in Cromwell's career, as he is named as the "Master of our Jewel House." Cromwell would rise to be Henry VIII's chief minister, and he became the instigator of Henry's English Reformation before his execution in 1540. *National Portrait Gallery, London, UK.*

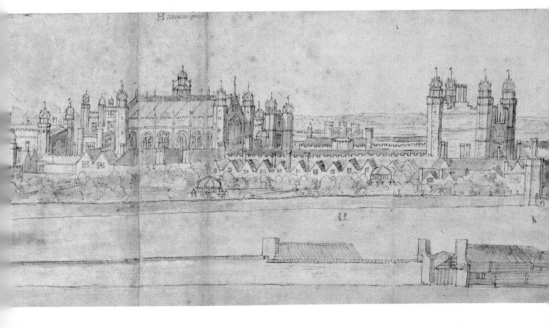

STEEVEN   GARDNER

TOP: Stephen Gardiner, Bishop of Winchester. A brilliant lawyer, Privy Councillor, and ambassador, the conservative Gardiner (*c*.1483–1555) accused the queen, Kateryn Parr, of heresy. He was later struck out of the list of executors and regency councillors that Henry VIII included in his last will and testament. *Oxburgh Hall, Norfolk, UK/ National Trust Photographic Library.* RIGHT: Thomas Howard, 3rd Duke of Norfolk, painted by Hans Holbein. The most senior member of the powerful Howard family and one of the premier noblemen in the country, Thomas Howard (1473–1554) bears, in the portrait, the symbols of his position as Earl Marshal of England. Norfolk was arrested on charges of high treason in December 1546 and was excluded from Henry VIII's last will and testament. *Heritage Images/ Getty Images.*

TOP: Sir Richard Southwell, painted by Holbein. A friend of the Earl of Surrey and a conservative in religion, Southwell (1518–64) may also have been responsible for Surrey's denunciation and subsequent arrest. He was appointed in King Henry's will to be an assistant to Edward's regency council. *DEA/G. Nimatallah/De Agostini/ Getty Images.* RIGHT: Sir William Herbert, painted by Hans Eworth. A dynamic soldier with a reputation for fiery behavior, Herbert (*c.*1501–70) was a favorite of Henry VIII and one of the Chief Gentlemen of the King's Privy Chamber. He was named in Henry's last will as an executor and regency councillor to Edward VI, who created him Earl of Pembroke in 1551. Herbert was also related by marriage to Henry—his first wife was Anne Parr, sister of Kateryn. © *Collection of the Earl of Pembroke, Wilton House, Wilts, UK/Bridgeman Images.*

LEFT: William Paulet, Lord St. John, in a portrait by an unknown artist. As Great Master of the King's Household and Lord President of the Privy Council, Paulet (*c.*1485–1572) was a longstanding servant of the king. He was named as a regency councillor and executor in Henry VIII's last will and testament. Seemingly flexible in religion, he was a great survivor through the vicissitudes of Tudor politics under successive reigns. © *National Portrait Gallery, London, UK.* BOTTOM: Sir Anthony Browne (d. 1548), Master of the King's Horse, in a portrait by an unknown sixteenth-century artist. It is augmented with biographical inscriptions. Browne, who was a close companion and servant of the king, was named as a regency councillor and executor in Henry VIII's last will and testament. It was Browne who, albeit unsuccessfully, objected to Stephen Gardiner's exclusion from the regency council. © *National Portrait Gallery, London, UK.*

Sir Thomas Seymour, in a posthumous painting, with verses of praise, by an unknown artist of the later sixteenth century. Younger brother of Edward Seymour (Earl of Hertford), Sir Thomas (1508–49) became, after Henry's death, Baron Seymour of Sudeley. On January 23, 1547, he was made a Privy Councillor. He had previously been named by Henry VIII as an assistant to the sixteen regency councillors in the king's last will and testament. In May 1547, Sir Thomas married the king's widow, Kateryn Parr—though his chief claim to fame, or notoriety, was his alleged plotting to marry Princess Elizabeth after Kateryn's death, which ensured his downfall. © *National Portrait Gallery, London, UK/Bridgeman Images.*

King Edward VI and the Pope (*c.*1575), by an unknown artist. This painting concocts a scene in which Henry VIII, on his deathbed, points to his successor in the shape of Prince Edward, thus commissioning the dramatic Protestant reformation that took place under Edward VI's reign. Under Edward's feet, the pope has been knocked over by a book declaring "The Word of the Lord endureth forever," while (top right) violent iconoclasts pull down images against a backdrop of destruction. The standing figure to Edward's right has been identified as Edward Seymour (Earl of Hertford, later Duke of Somerset and Lord Protector), while among the seated councillors are Archbishop Thomas Cranmer (in white) and, to his right, Lord Russell. Sir William Paget and John Dudley (Viscount Lisle, later Earl of Warwick) are also probably represented. © *National Portrait Gallery, London, UK.*

honour and surety of our said Sovereign Lord's person, or the advancement of his affairs."[17] They noted that having "reverently and diligently considered the great charge committed unto us," they had "fully resolved and agreed with one voice and consent . . . to stand to and maintain the said last will and testament of our said master . . . and every part and article of the same to the uttermost of our powers, wits and cunnings." A day later, they would swear oaths promising to uphold the will faithfully.[18]

This loyal adherence to the terms and conditions of the will did not, however, prevent them from concluding that for the honor and surety of the government—a reference to the carte-blanche clause in Henry's will empowering them to make any decisions they saw fit for this purpose—and to ensure order and direction in the king's affairs, "some special man . . . should be preferred" among them to be their leader. This person, they noted, should be one of "virtue, wisdom and experience," one able to be "a special remembrancer" and keep a certain account of all things, or else they might quickly fall into disorder and confusion. Who should this person be? Of course, it should be Edward's only blood relative on the Council, the Earl of Hertford, whom they gave "first and chief place among us" and "the name and title of Protector of all the realms and dominions of the King's Majesty."[19]

Hertford and Paget had executed their plan beautifully. In so doing, had they breached Henry's will, by breaking the terms of an equal and unified government by council that Henry had decreed? Historians have been divided over whether or not the events of January 31—just three days after Henry's death—constituted a violation of both the spirit and letter of the will, or a perfectly acceptable implementation of its provisions.[20] The councillors themselves swore that they had abided by Henry's terms, for Hertford became Protector with their "one whole assent, concord and agreement" and on "this special and express condition" that "he shall not do any act but with the advice and consent of the rest of the co-executors," according to the terms of the will.[21]

A thin veneer of legitimacy had been maintained. But it was soon to be entirely shattered.

9

The "Unwritten Will"

T he power that Hertford and Paget acquired on Henry VIII's death rested entirely on the late king's will. It did not rest, however, just on their status within it as executors and regency councillors. Instead, their ability to grasp the opportunity offered to them depended on the gifts left to them by the king, those both written and unwritten.

After his lengthy list of provisions for the succession and his naming of the executors, Henry, in conformity now with other royal wills, made his bequests. He charged his executors to pay and fulfill any outstanding debts and promises, and he explained how his property should be divided. This was mostly straightforward: there are frustratingly few personal gifts, and we search largely in vain for the legacies of individual items and statements of affection found in many wills of the period, such as Stephen Gardiner's effusive donation to Queen Mary I in his will, which stated that he could in no part recompense her great favor to him "if I should live many lives [so] I have and do for witness thereof leave unto her a cup of gold with a sapphire in the top" or his bequest to "my Lord

Legate's Grace a ring with a diamante, not so big as he is worthy to have," or Kateryn Parr's bequest of all her possessions to her fourth husband, Sir Thomas Seymour, "wishing them to be a thousand times more in value than they were."[1] Henry VIII's is far more prosaic; but what is interesting is what the will hints at but does not say—what has come to be known as Henry's "unwritten will."

Henry VIII did have certain stated destinations for his great wealth, however, which give us an insight into whom, and what, he held dear. In total, he left bequests to sixty-six individuals. He gave the responsibility for ensuring these were given out to Sir Edmund Peckham, who had been cofferer (treasurer) of the royal household since 1524 (folio 17).

His son Edward was the main beneficiary. Henry bequeathed him "all our plate, stuff of household, artillery, ordnance, munitions, ships, cabettes and all other things and implements to them belonging, and money also and jewels" (folio 19)—everything, in short, that he had not gifted to someone else in the will.[2] When Henry died, an inventory was made of his possessions, across all his palaces, and its recent editors estimate that the total value of his gift to Edward was worth around £1,200,000 in 1547: an extraordinarily huge bequest.[3] Its 17,813 itemized entries include 9,150 guns, cannons, or other pieces of artillery; over 2,000 pieces of tapestry; 2,028 pieces of plate; jewelery; armor; books, including volumes by Aquinas, Augustine, Cicero, Livy, Seneca, and Erasmus, and New Testaments in English, Latin, and French, along with many primers, prayer books, and books of songs; horses; salt clocks; maps; chandlery; carpets; perfumes; regalia; ships; the crown imperial; medical equipment; gemstones; paintings; globes; miniatures; games; ivory; musical instruments; mother of pearl; spice holders; mirrors; goblets; toys; furnishings; terracotta; embroidery; carvings; and all items from the king's wardrobe. There was even "a piece of a unicorn's horn" (see Appendix III for more highlights).[4]

The ostensible condition for Edward's receipt of this enormous inheritance was a solemn order to be bound by the advice of Henry's nominated councillors in all matters:

> *. . . charging and commanding him on pain of our curse, seeing*
> *that he hath so loving a father of us and that our chief labour*
> *and study in this world is to establish him in the crown impe-*
> *rial of this realm after our decease . . . that he be ordered and*
> *ruled both in his marriage and also in ordering of the affairs*
> *of the realm as well outward as inward, and also in all his*
> *own private affairs, and in giving of offices of charge by the*
> *advice and counsel of our right entirely beloved councillors*
> (folios 19 and 20)

Edward could have everything, but the price was total submission to the councillors whom Henry believed would continue to enact his will.

To his daughters—technically illegitimate but still his nonetheless— Henry bequeathed "money, plate, jewels and household stuff" to the value of £10,000 each (folio 24), although he left it to the discretion of his executors as to whether this should be a larger sum, or even a smaller one should his daughters fail to heed his councillors' advice on whom to marry. In addition, "from the first hour of our death" until their marriages— responsibility for finding them honorable spouses being given to the councillors—Mary and Elizabeth were to be furnished with £3,000 a year to live on (folio 25). This was a conventional bequest; Henry VII had made similar provision for Mary Tudor in 1509 (although he had left her a much more generous £50,000 for her dowry or if her planned marriage were not effected).[5]

Provision was also made for his wife and queen, Kateryn Parr, as reward for her "great love, obedience, chasteness of life and wisdom." She was to receive "plate, jewels and household stuff" to the value of £3,000, "such apparel as it shall please her to take of such as she has already," £1,000 in cash, and her "dower and jointer" according to the grant made by Act of Parliament, which included the manors of Hanworth and Chelsea (folio 25).

The next set of beneficiaries were Henry's executors, who, "for the kindness and good service" they had showed the king, each received some few hundred pounds. Wriothesley, Lord St. John, Russell, Hertford, and Lisle all received the most: money or lands to the value of £500 each. Paget, Denny, Herbert, Montagu, Bromley, North, and the Wottons accrued £300 each. Archbishop Cranmer, who is mentioned first, was to receive 500 marks—so around £333; it is not clear why his amount was unique.[6]

Those others who benefited from Henry's will were his trusted royal servants. He notes that his bequests were because of "the special love and favour that we bear to our trusty councillors and other our said servants hereafter" (folio 26). To each of the assistants to the councillors, he left £200—with one exception: Sir William Petre, one of his principal secretaries, does not appear to have received any bequest. As the assistants are named amid a host of other people, this may just have been an unfortunate oversight.

Many of Henry's legatees were his court favorites. Sir Thomas Darcy, Sir Thomas Speke, Sir Philip Hoby, Sir Thomas Paston, Sir Maurice Berkeley, Sir Ralph Sadler, Sir Thomas Cawarden, Sir Peter Mewtas, and Sir Edward Bellingham were all Gentlemen of the King's Privy Chamber, who had served Henry in war—mostly in the French campaigns of 1540s, but also in Scotland.[7] All received sums of either £200 or 200 marks (£133 6s 8d). The only other person to receive this great a sum was Thomas Audley, who seems to have been the brother of the late Thomas, Baron Audley of Walden, Henry's former lord chancellor.

All ten witnesses to the will received bequests. Most of the gentlemen and grooms of the Privy Chamber—Henry Nevill, William Saint-Barbe, Richard Coke, and David Vincent—and the three royal physicians—doctors George Owen, Thomas Wendy, and Robert Huicke—received amounts of £100 each. John Gates, as a member of the Privy Chamber and one of the clerks responsible for Henry's dry stamp, received £200; Edmund Harman, as a Groom of the Privy Chamber and the king's barber-surgeon, received 200 marks. The servant, or possible apothecary, Patrick ("Patrec") received only 100 marks.

The remaining beneficiaries, most of whom also received 100 marks, seem to have been less elevated royal servants. Among them are James

A sketch by Holbein, showing the wise old John, Lord Russell (*c.*1485–1555), Lord Privy Seal. A member of Henry VIII's Privy Council, he was also named by Henry as an executor and regency councillor to Edward. He was later created Earl of Bedford. Russell probably chose to be depicted with his left side facing the viewer, because his right eye had been damaged in battle. *Royal Collection Trust © Her Majesty Queen Elizabeth II, 2015/Bridgeman Images.*

Rufforth, "Keeper of our House here" at Westminster; Richard Cecil, "Yeoman of our Robes"; and Thomas Sternhold, "Groom of our Robes" (folio 27). One of the most human aspects of the will lies in the fact that Henry could not remember everyone's names perfectly: there is a blank space before Sternhold's surname, as before Coke's, and in the case of his apothecary, Thomas Alsopp, and four of his servants—John Ailef, Richard Ferrers, Henry Forrest, and John Holland—Henry managed either the first name or the surname, but not both. Finally, after leaving £50 each to the "four huissiers [ushers] of our chamber, being daily waiters," Henry instructed his executors to pay a legacy to any of his ordinary servants they thought "meet" (appropriate) but whom he had not named (folio 27).

These payments do seem to have been honored by Edward VI's new regency council, but they were not the only grants and gifts claimed by them.[8]

The instruction to Henry's executors to confer rewards on his servants as they saw fit helps contextualize a clause in the will that (as discussed earlier) has been the source of much controversy:

> . . . we will that all such grants and gifts as we have given or promised to any, which be not yet perfected . . . as they ought to be . . . and all such recompenses for exchanges, sales or any other thing or things, as ought to have been made by use and be not yet accomplished, shall be perfected (folio 18)

Known as the "unfulfilled gifts clause," this instructed that any intended gifts, grants, or payments, which Henry had promised but not realized before death, ought to be honored. It was one of the sentences that some historians have thought must have been inserted into the will in order to give leverage to the Hertford clique—although, as shown earlier, it could not have been added after the will's composition and redrafting. It is also unnecessary to imagine such secret intrigue. Rather, the clause was a standard insertion in medieval royal wills, because the idea of failing to honor a promised gift brought shame and dishonor to the one who had pledged it.[9] It is probably this clause that was evoked to ensure the foundation of Christ's Hospital and Trinity College, Cambridge, both of which Henry endowed in his last months.[10] There were also many other gifts of manors and lands granted by the king before his death—such as the grant of lands to Sir Thomas Cawarden and his wife, Elizabeth in December 1546, which included lands in Lingfield (in Surrey), a water-mill called Newland Mill, the manors of Hexsted and "Byllesherst" (perhaps Billingshurst), an inn called the Green Dragon in Southwark, and many others properties besides—and this clause probably smoothed the way to their accomplishment.[11]

The reason this clause has seemed suspect is because it also proved highly convenient to those in power after Henry's death. It enabled Hertford to claim the title "Duke of Somerset" and the position of Earl Marshal of England, and allowed the granting of peerages and baronies, offices and valuable gifts of lands to councillors and courtiers, including Lisle, Wriothesley, Seymour, Rich, and William Parr, Earl of Essex.

Nevertheless, there is reason to believe the story Paget told about the legacies in Henry VIII's "unwritten will." On Monday February 6, 1547, just over a week after Henry's death, Paget reported to the assembled Council that after the arrest of Surrey and Norfolk in December, Henry had discussed with his secretary, in the presence of Sir John Gates, how to redistribute the Howard lands, "thinking it expedient that the same should be liberally dispersed and given to diverse noble men and others His Majesty's good servants."[12] In addition, Henry had, according to Paget, reflected on the fact that the nobility of the country "was greatly decayed" and, thinking to advance some to higher places of honor, had asked Paget to write a list of suggested names. This is plausible. Certainly, the Tudor nobility was looking somewhat depleted: there had been no Earl of

Warwick since 1499, no Duke of Buckingham since 1521, no Earl of Lincoln since 1534, no Earl or Marquess of Pembroke, nor Duke of Somerset since the deaths of Anne Boleyn—created Marquess of Pembroke—and Henry Fitzroy in 1536, no Earl of Northumberland since Sir Henry Percy's death in 1537, and no Earl of Southampton since Sir William Fitzwilliam's death in 1542. And Henry was just about to destroy the Duke of Norfolk too. The old king might well have considered the time ripe to swell the ranks of the English aristocracy.

Paget states that he therefore prepared a list of those whom he thought meet, proposing Hertford to be a duke; Essex to be a marquess; Lisle, St. John, Russell, and Wriothesley to be earls; and ten knights, including Sir Thomas Seymour, to be barons. He also advised the king to accompany the titles with such liberality in the way of lands that the recipients might be able to uphold the honor of their new ranks, and redistributed the Howard offices of state. Paget suggested lands worth one thousand marks (£666 13s 4d) a year for Hertford, £200 a year for Lisle and so on, and Henry instructed Paget to sound out the intended beneficiaries on the quiet to check that no one had any objections. Paget then recalled to Henry some others whom His Majesty "was minded before to be good to," including Denny, whose "painful" (painstaking) daily service Paget remembered to the king, and their names were added to the list.[13]

At some later date, the matter was reviewed, and it was found that, for three reasons, the initial list of promotions needed to be revised. Paget's conversations revealed that some wanted to stay in their current ranks, while others complained that the money was insufficient. The Duke of Norfolk declared that he wanted his lands to go to Prince Edward, and Henry's increasingly pressing sense of mortality drove him to favor some over others, for he wanted, said Paget, to "place us all about his son as men whom he trusted and loved above all other specially." So an amended proposal was drawn up. "When I had made it and read it to him," Paget notes, "he took it off me and put [it] in his pocket, and upon my request was content I should declare unto every man what was by His Majesty determined . . . and so I did and all were pleased."[14]

The matter had been decided, but the king had then died before the changes could be driven through. So, knowing that in Henry's will he had stated that "whatsoever should in any wise appear to his Council to have been promised by him, the same should be performed," on February 6 Paget urged the assembled councillors to abide by this condition and grant the titles, offices, and lands as laid out by the late king.[15] The Council declared itself bound in conscience to obey the will, and on February 15 the new titles were announced. The creations proceeded on the following day, and lands were distributed a week later.[16]

Some historians have rather doubted Paget's version of events. They have noted how very well Hertford did out of the proposals, and suspected Paget of manipulating Henry into offering advancements to Hertford and his supporters—those evangelicals who would support Hertford's elevation as Protector—as ballast for their coup. If they do not believe that the "unfulfilled gifts clause" was added later, they surmise that the king had little idea of the full significance or consequences of the clause when it was agreed.[17]

Yet, we have evidence to substantiate Paget's testimony. In the State Papers in the National Archives, we have his first list, in a clear clerical hand.[18] We can see Paget's original tally of thirteen peerage promotions, more than half of them complete with grants of land, plus ten other appointments to offices vacated by the Howards.[19] We can also clearly identify crossings-through, interstitial additions, marginalia, and other amendments and annotations in Paget's own more spidery script. These are evidently the changes to the list that emerged from Paget's conversations and Henry's intervention: they have the scribbled feel of emendations made on the hoof as Paget sat talking with Henry. The documentary evidence seems to uphold Paget's story.

It is true that the list and the revisions did benefit Hertford and some of those close to him. To the lands worth £666 13s 4d for Hertford were added new land grants to the value of £1,100 a year. Sir Thomas Seymour's acquisition of a barony and £300 a year was inflated to £500 a year. Wriothesley, who was to be an earl, saw the value of his land grant increase

Sir William Paget's original list of thirteen peerage promotions, written in another clerical hand. Over this, a more spidery second hand—Paget's own—shows his amendments, with crossings-through, interstitial additions and marginalia, perhaps made on the hoof as he sat talking with Henry. *The National Archives.*

from £100 to £300 a year. Lisle's money increased by £100 a year. In the margin, Paget had added the names of Denny, Herbert, Cawarden, and Gates, with financial benefits attached to each. Yet, this is not the full story. The earldoms originally proposed for Russell and St. John and the barony for Sir Thomas Arundel were scrapped. The offer of a dukedom for Hertford was also amended: rather than simply saying he would be made Duke of Hertford and his son Earl of Wiltshire, it now read: "Hertford to be . . . Duke of Somerset or Exeter or Hertford and his son Earl of Wiltshire if he be Duke of Hertford." Hertford therefore had to choose: he could either have a dukedom with royal precedents—the last Duke of Somerset had been Henry's illegitimate son, who had died at the age of seventeen—or he could have an earldom for his son: not both. It would be illogical to conclude that these changes were solely made to the benefit of those who would vote in the regency council for Hertford's protectorate; of the regency councillors, only Russell, St. John, Lisle, and Wriothesley were proposed for promotion, and two of them lost out with the revisions.[20] Moreover, contrary to the rumors that Van der Delft heard about future promotions, Paget himself received no title, grant, or new office.[21]

Rather than inferring that the amendments were made by Paget to garner support for his dear friend, Hertford, to be Protector, we should instead consider, given the evidential corroboration, that Paget was perhaps telling the truth: that Henry had oversight of this entire process and did fully intend these advancements, even if Paget had some influence over the proceedings. The fact that Hertford was made to choose between his own higher prestige or a double peerage for his family smacks of Henry; as Professor Eric Ives put it, it "looks like Henry making his brother-in-law pay for his ambition."[22] It may be simply the fact too that Russell, St. John, and Arundel refused their creations as Paget reported, and that the size of the grants was increased (to a total of £2,266 13s 4d a year) because, as people said, they were previously insufficient to uphold the new ranks.[23] We cannot be sure that Henry dictated Paget's changes, but it seems very likely. Henry VIII's "unwritten will" seems intended by the king to reward those around him who would have care of the government of his son.

William Parr (1513–71), Earl of Essex and Marquess of Northampton. This half-finished chalk and ink sketch by Holbein shows the good looks of Kateryn Parr's brother. He had grown up in the household of Henry VIII's illegitimate son, Henry Fitzroy, Duke of Richmond and Somerset, and risen at court with his sister's favor. In April 1543, William Parr was made a Knight of the Garter. A member of Henry VIII's Privy Council, he was nominated as an assistant to the regency council to Edward VI in Henry's last will. *Royal Collection Trust © Her Majesty Queen Elizabeth II, 2015 / Bridgeman Images.*

The new government duly handed out the promotions and rewards in Edward VI's name. Although entirely to be expected, it is notable that the tone of the proclamation reflects Paget's account precisely and very much suggests that the preferments were Henry's intention. It states "considering that divers of his counsellors and princes were not gratified and rewarded by him [Henry VIII] according to their worth," "for the great zeal [and] tender love" Henry had for them, "for the advancement of the common weal," and to "maintain and advance the estate and degree of nobility," the late king thought it best to honor a number of his councillors, "such personages as the highness intended to advance."[24] The scheme was Henry's, one he was "minded resolved and fully determined" to carry out. There is every reason why such a tone should have been employed in this proclamation even if Henry had no such intentions, and, of course, Paget represented the government; but the level of consonance between Paget's story to the Council and this proclamation, and its repetition again in the Calendar of Patent Rolls, which notes the fulfilment of these grants, is striking.[25]

Many in the new government stood to benefit from the changes. From February 16, 1547, Hertford became not only Lord Protector, but also the Duke of Somerset. William Parr, Earl of Essex became the Marquess of Northampton; Lisle became Earl of Warwick; Wriothesley, Earl of Southampton; Sir Thomas Seymour, Baron Seymour of Sudeley, and Sir Richard Rich, Baron Rich of Leeze. It makes sense that the minutes of the Privy Council from February 23, when the lands were parceled out, are replete with the language of duty and obedience to Henry VIII's will, and especially to his clause about unfulfilled promises: the councillors are bound, they assert, to do what the will instructs, and loath to do any acts unwarranted by it.[26] They exaggerate how beholden they are to Henry's will—and the consequence is the enrichment of many of their number. At this stage, both reality and rhetoric combined in acquiescence to Henry's will.

Within a month, however, Edward VI's government had thrown off the shackles of Henry VIII's will and buried the testament along with their late monarch.

IO

The Legacy of the Will

E dward VI was crowned on February 20, 1547. Between his
arrival at the Tower, at the very end of January, and his proces-
sion from the Tower of London to Westminster, on the day
before the coronation, he had waited for three weeks, while "in the mean
season the Council sat every day for the performance of the will."[1] Much
of this enactment of Henry's will involved the fulfilling of bequests, the
arrangement of offices, and the distribution of titles. During this time,
the first minor betrayal of Henry VIII's will took place: within five days
of the king's death, Sir Thomas Seymour had been advanced from his
position as an assistant to the councillors and appointed as a seventeenth
regency councillor. It was clear, nevertheless, to foreign observers, like
Van der Delft, that there was a core to the Council who were really running the show: "there are four who . . . will take into their hands the
entire direction of affairs." Hertford and Lisle, Van der Delft thought,
would enjoy the "honours and titles of rulers of the realm," but Wriothesley
and Paget "will in reality have the entire management of affairs," for

"without these two they can do but little."[2] As usual, Van der Delft was only half right. Very soon, one of these four would be toppled, and this ousting represented the first major and undeniable breach in the conditions laid out by Henry VIII's will.

Thomas Wriothesley had ostensibly supported Hertford's elevation to the protectorate as a first among equals—yet scraps of evidence suggest that he had been less than happy about Hertford's promotion and was determined to keep the Protector's authority to the terms of Henry VIII's will. A manuscript by an unknown author in the British Library records a quarrel between Wriothesley and Hertford in early February, and states that "Wriothesley was sore against him to be made Protector."[3] As lord chancellor, Wriothesley was keeper of the Great Seal of England, which needed to be attached to every royal patent and commission; in short, Wriothesley had a veto on all appointments to sinecures and offices.[4] He controlled the distribution of power and the acquisition of wealth; he could prevent the new Duke of Somerset from wielding the authority he wanted. He also disagreed with the Protector's stance on matters of religion, when the dramatic Protestant iconoclasm of Somerset's premiership would become the defining characteristic of Edward's reign. Two days before Edward's coronation, Wriothesley, now Earl of Southampton, blundered, and his misstep was sufficiently grave for Somerset to be able to eject him from the machinery of power.

Southampton's error was that, keen to focus on the business of government in the Council, he had delegated his responsibilities in Chancery to four experienced civil lawyers who were to hear cases in his absence. This essentially constituted a commission to others to act as lord chancellor without the king's consent. On March 5, he was charged at Westminster before the rest of the Council with having "made manifold abuses in the Court of Chancery . . . to the great hindrance, prejudice and decay of the contrary to the common laws of the realm."[5] In so doing, it was found that he had "offend[ed] the King's Majesty" and, by the common law, "forfeit[ed] his office as chancellor."[6] He was to be fined and imprisoned under house arrest, at the king's will.

This wonderful sketch, by Hans Holbein, portrays Lord Chancellor Thomas Wriothesley (1505–50). A member of Henry VIII's Privy Council, Wriothesley was also nominated by the king as an executor and regency councillor to Edward VI. He was later created Earl of Southampton. A conservative in religion, Wriothesley racked Anne Askewe with his own hands in 1546 (as did Richard Rich). He was soon deposed by the Earl of Hertford's Protestant government—although Wriothesley, in turn, later helped dismantle Somerset's protectorate. © *RMN-Grand Palais (Musée du Louvre).*

This infraction was genuine, but it was not Southampton's real offense. That lay in his opposition to Somerset's position, as hinted at in his trial when Somerset stated that Southampton had "used unfitting words to me, the said Protector, to the prejudice of the king's estate and the hindrance of his Majesty's affairs."[7] Somerset's alleged concern about "what danger might ensue to the King's most royal person, and what hindrance, detriment and subversion to his affairs" should the Great Seal remain in the possession of "so stout and arrogant a person as durst and would presume at his will and pleasure to seal things that he might by any liberty, custom, privilege or other grant by virtue of his office" sounds like a serious case of transference.[8] The Great Seal passed to Lord St. John's keeping, and Southampton fell from grace.

The deposition of one of Henry VIII's nominated councillors was the beginning of the end of any adherence to Henry's will. On March 12, it was overthrown entirely. Letters patent were issued, with the Great Seal attached and in the king's name, which gave Somerset power over the royal prerogative and the right to appoint the members of the King's Council.[9] The regency councillors and assistant councillors named in the will were combined to form one single Privy Council, and Henry's prudent schema was quashed. In practice, however, the composition of the Council was moot, for Somerset proceeded to rule as an autocrat, jettisoning all Henry's hopes for balanced, conciliar rule.

A Royal Commission on March 21, written in Edward VI's name, confirmed Somerset's singular standing. It nominated and appointed one "meet and trusty personage above all others," agreeing to "ratify, approve, confirm, allow all and every thing and things whatsoever devised, set forth, committed and done by our said uncle as Governor of our person and Protector of our said realms and dominions."[10] Somerset had full and total control. That these were little short of regal powers is confirmed in the much later letter of Paget to Somerset in July 1549, when Paget reminded his master that "Your Grace is, during the king's young age of imperfection, to do his own things, as it were a king, and have His Majesty's absolute power." For inspiration of how to act, Paget would charge Somerset to look to the example of "him which died last, of most noble memory King Henry VIII."[11]

Henry's memory might have been dredged up when convenient to give an example of how to rule, but seldom can a monarch of such terrible power have been so quickly forgotten. Within eight weeks of Henry's death, the careful plan he had made for the future of the constitution had been entirely discarded. The "singular trust and special confidence" he had placed in his "right entirely beloved councillors" had been utterly misplaced.[12]

⬥

Henry VIII's will was not yet quite a dead duck; it continued to be evoked or contested throughout the sixteenth century in order to bolster claims to power, and—despite the best efforts of his children to overturn it—it so happened that the Tudor succession paralleled Henry's intentions.

In the first year of Edward VI's reign, an inscription by Edward's lord chancellor endorsing Henry VIII's will was added as a covering folio to the testament (see page 140). After Southampton's disgrace, the chancellorship was filled by Baron Rich: he may have tortured Anne Askewe back in 1546, but now, bending like a reed in the wind, he had repositioned himself as part of the new Protestant government under Somerset. But Somerset's power was not to last.

In October 1549, it was Henry VIII's will that provided the legal authority to Somerset's fellow Privy Councillors to dismantle his protectorate in a bloodless coup. Somerset's arrogant usurpation of the role of Lord Protector had not been to everyone's taste, and over the succeeding two years he grew increasingly autocratic and dismissive of his peers, while seeking popularity among the masses.[13] His tendency toward unilateral decision-making and pretensions to royal status (he adopted the royal "we") caused offense and convinced most members of the Privy Council that, despite being the king's most senior male relative, he was unfit for office. The coup was ostensibly led by the Earl of Southampton—briefly restored to power—but the power behind it came from Somerset's erstwhile ally John Dudley, Earl of Warwick. The charge against Somerset contained no suggestion that he had tampered with Henry VIII's will; there was, however, every suggestion that he had ignored its instructions.[14] Warwick succeeded Somerset, and although his more conciliar style of government positioned him as the first among equals—he never arrogated to himself the position of Lord Protector—in October 1551 he was elevated to the Dukedom of Northumberland. Days later, Somerset was arrested and subsequently executed on a technicality.

When Edward VI was dying in 1553, the fifteen-year-old king attempted to use his "device for the succession" to override the succession carefully outlined by Henry VIII. Following the "Protestant revolution" of his reign, Edward was desperate not to hand the throne to his Catholic half-sister Mary. His other reason for excluding her was that she was also technically illegitimate, since Henry had never relegitimized his daughters—despite naming them in his will, and in Acts of Parliament, as his successors. Ironically, in preparing his device, Edward was adopting his father's approach to the succession: it was in the gift of the king, and so what one monarch had given, another could take away. Edward's single-page device was a miniature imitation of Henry VIII's will.

In the document, Edward VI initially nominated only male heirs from the line of Henry VIII's younger sister, Mary—overlooking the line from Henry's elder sister, Margaret, as Henry himself had done. But when, in the spring of 1553, Edward realized that his illness was terminal, he inserted the crucial words "Lady Jane and her" before "heirs males," and so nominated as his direct heir his Protestant cousin Lady Jane Grey.[15] Some of Henry's former councillors, including Russell and St. John, raised objections to the casual disregard of Henry's will; but letters patent embodying Edward's device (which, under the terms of Henry's Acts of Succession, would have been legally sufficient to determine the succession) were drawn up by Lord Chief Justice Sir Edward Montagu—another of those that Henry had named for the regency council—and no fewer than 102 witnesses added their support to the final "declaration," which was also signed and sealed by the king.[16] This declaration was just passing through Parliament when Edward died.

During the abortive reign of Lady Jane Grey that followed, a letter from Mary on July 9, 1553, stating her claim to the throne, made specific reference to her right "by Act of Parliament and the testament and last will of our late dearest father King Henry the Eight."[17] Thus, while Edward had acted according to his father's precedent of writing his will, Mary espoused Henry's wishes as expressed within it: in each case, Henry VIII's will remained the lodestone.

Mary's adherence to her father's will in defense of her own accession, and her subsequent absence of "issue" after marriage in 1554, left her little choice but to pass the imperial crown down the line of succession that Henry had specified—to her half-sister, Elizabeth. Elizabeth's ill-concealed Protestantism meant that Mary resisted naming her as successor when she drew up her own will; but ten days before she died, the queen consented to the Council's request to make "certain declarations in favour of the Lady Elizabeth concerning the accession."[18] Within six hours of Mary's death, Elizabeth was proclaimed queen. Henry VIII's unlikely plan for the succession had now been fulfilled through three of his imagined scenarios.

A few years into Elizabeth I's reign, supporters of the Stuart claim to the throne, seeking to nominate Mary, Queen of Scots as the natural successor to Elizabeth, tried to dispute the validity of Henry VIII's will. Sir William Maitland, Lord of Lethington and Secretary of Scotland, wrote to Sir William Cecil, Elizabeth's first minister, on January 4, 1566 calling Henry's last will a "dissembled and forged signed testament."[19] In an argument also advanced at some length in certain manuscripts from the 1560s, including an anonymous treatise of 1566 (possibly written by Edward Plowden), Henry's will was declared to be invalid because it was signed by dry stamp, and not "with his most gracious hand" as specified by the Acts of Succession.[20] This lack of signature led the anonymous author to conclude "that if his will in writing be not signed with his hand, it is insufficient to make the crown pass," "the authority of the act is not executed and so

Edward VI's "device for the succession," written in his youthful hand. Just as Henry VIII had done in his will, King Edward VI wanted to exercise his monarchical right to nominate his successor. Edward initially named "L" Jane's heires masles" [Lady Jane's heirs males], choosing his successors from the line of Henry VIII's younger sister, Mary. But, when he realized that he was dying, he made a crucial change, turning "Jane's" into "Jane" and following it with the words "and her," so that he bequeathed his throne directly to Lady Jane Grey and, only then, to her male heirs. *Inner Temple Library.*

the limitation of the crown by that will is void."[21] In short, if the will could be proved insufficiently endorsed by Henry VIII, its exclusion of the Scottish line descended from Henry's sister, Margaret, from the crown of England could no longer stand.

Yet, Elizabeth I's long life gradually erased the need for this argument. When she died, the crown would indeed pass down the Scottish line that Henry had excluded, and James VI of Scotland would also rule as James I of England. Henry VIII's will had finally ceased to have any consequence at all.

——❖——

There are many stories about the fate of Henry VIII's will. In 1547, it was placed in the Treasury for safekeeping, stored in a "round box or bag of black velvet."[22] This must be the original that now resides in the National Archives at Kew.

Other copies, however, existed. Bishop Cuthbert Tunstal, as one of Henry's executors, had one. When he died in November 1559, his belongings were sent to Westminster, and Matthew Parker, Elizabeth I's newly nominated Archbishop of Canterbury, discovered among them "two small caskets, where I think [there is] no great substance either of money or of writing. There is one roll of books . . . which is nothing else but King Henry's testament."[23] Another copy was kept by the treasurer, Sir Edmund Peckham, and inherited by his son, who gave it to a servant with firm instructions to keep it safe and "let no man look in it." The servant was not so circumspect. He later admitted that he had put the will "in a basket with other writings in the chamber where I and three other of my fellows lay, using the same basket also to put in our apparel and other necessaries so much as it would hold, having to the same neither lock nor key."[24]

In the end, both literally and metaphorically, Henry VIII's last will and testament had become just another scrap in the wastepaper basket.

Epilogue

To some, Henry VIII's last will and testament is "the epitome of his reign" in that, by being "determined by other intelligences and shaped for other purposes" than those of the king, it demonstrates the way that Henry's "persona was a mask through which spoke the king's servants more often than the king himself."[1] The foregoing chapters have outlined why I think that this judgment is largely mistaken and have attempted to show that Henry VIII was not the marionette of his servants in the matter of the making of his will—nor in anything else.

Henry's will does, however, epitomize his reign in a number of ways. Its focus is identical to the "chief labour and study" of Henry's life: the pursuit of a stable succession in order to preserve the dynasty. Just as the central features of Henry's reign derived from his desire to ensure an heir, so the majority of the will was devoted to planning for the security of his son's reign and to making provision for nine possible eventualities. In these preparations, Henry offered idiosyncratic, but practical plans: the line of succession was to exclude the Stuart line descending from his sister Margaret; the form of government to see young Edward through the perilous and unstable time of the minority was to be a regency council of sixteen, who would, with full and unfettered power, rule as a union of equals until Edward reached the age of eighteen.

The will also neatly represents Henry's religious outlook—a conservative orthodoxy in key areas of doctrine, coupled with an adherence to his new article of faith: his own position as Supreme Head of the Church. While there is much religiosity in the will, there is, however, little sense of a personal relationship with the Divine beyond that of one monarch addressing another. In this, it betrays another prominent feature of Henry's character: the self-involved nature of his relationship with God and the world.

There is, however, something rather touching about the optimism and naivety of the will. That Henry believed that Kateryn Parr yet might bear him sons, that he might yet marry again, and that his councillors, in whom he placed so much trust, would be faithful to his wishes, is testament to his hubristic arrogance and his incredible capacity for self-delusion, but also to his buoyancy of spirit and his faith in the genuine devotion of those around him. What is most striking is the disjuncture between his profound belief that he would be obeyed and loved—that even after death, he would leave a forceful imprint on his closest companions—and the reality that they so quickly, and thoroughly, shrugged him off.

⬥

The rash and rapid way in which his former councillors crushed Henry's careful plans for Edward VI's minority and propelled themselves into power has made it all too easy for historians to apply the benefits of hindsight to the question of the composition of the will. The lightning success of Hertford and Paget in securing control after Henry's death leads naturally to the assumption that well before Henry expired, a cabal must have been conspiring to stage a coup. But Dr. Glyn Redworth was right to argue that, instead, Hertford "did not so much seize power as inherit it."[2] Hertford and Paget did make plans for Hertford's elevation and Paget's place at his side, but only, according to Paget's own private account, on the night of

Henry's death. To do so before would have been recklessly dangerous in an age when words could be treasonous. It was only at this final juncture—when Henry looked certain not to rally once more—that they could talk, in whispers, of how to proceed when the "old fox" finally breathed his last. H. G. Wells wrote of Queen Victoria that she "was like a great paper-weight that for half a century sat upon men's minds, and when she was removed their ideas began to blow about all over the place haphazardly." So, too, Henry's imminent death permitted his courtiers to think the unthinkable.

Henry VIII's last will and testament was the product of his own mastery during his last months of life. Until those final hours, he remained powerful and in charge: we see evidence of Henry's close involvement and thorough direction of both the sidelining of the willful Gardiner from the regency council and the destruction of the sycophantic Norfolk and his foolhardy son.

The Edwardian government would go on to be so religiously zealous that it has also been tempting to read evangelicalism into the motivations of Henry's councillors; but there is precious little evidence of a religiously motivated operation at work in the last season of Henry's life. Instead, the possibly evangelical Surrey was probably condemned on the word of a conservative friend, Southwell, while the conservative Lord Chancellor Wriothesley remained at the heart of the Council until his deposition in March 1547, despite having driven the hunt for heretics the previous summer and even racking Anne Askewe with his own hands.

Nor was the will a product of forgeries and later alterations for the aggrandizement of Hertford and friends. It is physically impossible that the will, as it stands, had sentences inserted into its text, and there is no evidence to support the hypothesis of its later alteration. The explanation for its inclusion in the January list of documents signed by dry stamp is far more innocent: its inclusion was designed to proclaim its authenticity.

Henry VIII's last will was, in short, not the result of a conspiracy but of Henry's own volition. It was precisely as he intended it to be.

Henry's "unwritten will"—the grant of titles, lands, and offices to many of those in his government—similarly also seems to bear his imprint. As boons to persuade Hertford's fellow councillors to vote for his protectorate it would have been fairly ineffectual; in tone, it is Henrician, providing—as with the devising of the regency council—for the government of his son.

In the month after Henry died, his councillors protested fulsomely and at length that they would see Henry's last will and testament "duly and wholly accomplished and fulfilled as to their most bounden duties appertaineth." In reality, the clause enabling the distribution of the benefits of the unwritten will was one of the only ones that that they really felt compelled to keep.[3] Within weeks, all Henry's provisions for the governance of the realm had been completely overturned.

Henry's trust in his beloved councillors was ill rewarded. But, ultimately, he put his faith in a higher power. Four times in his will (folios 9, 16, 18 and 23) he required his executors "truly and fully to see this my Last Will performed in all things" and "observed and kept forever perpetually" "as they will answer before Almighty God at the dreadful Day of Judgement." Henry had made provision for their failure; they would get their just deserts. Ever confident of his ability to command the ineffable, he was sure that Almighty God would have his back covered.

APPENDIX I

Henry VIII's Last Will and Testament: A Transcription

The text shown here is a transcription of the will as it exists in the National Archives, Kew, under the reference E/23/4. The transcription that appears in Thomas Rymer's documentary collection *Foedera* (third edition, 1739–45; Volume XV, pp. 142–5) is largely accurate, but it follows the eighteenth-century practice of superfluous capitalization and includes quite a number of minor misreadings, unwarranted corrections and mistranscriptions.[1]

In this transcription, the original spelling is maintained. Although not all proper names are capitalized in the original, they have been here. Where punctuation has been added to aid reading, this appears within square brackets. Carets [ʌ] have been added before and after text that is in superscript in the will.

[FOLIO 1]

Henry R
In the name of God and of the glorious and blessed
Virgin our Lady Sainct Mary and of all the holy
company of Heaven. We Henry[,] by the grace
of God[,] King of England Fraunce and Irlande[,]
Defendeur of the Faith, and in erth ymedyately
under God the Supreme Hed of the Church of
England and Irland of that name th[']eight,
calling to our remembraunce the great giftes and
benefites of Almighty God given unto us in this
transitory lief[,] give unto him our moost lowly
and humble thankes, knowledging our self insufficient
in any part to deserve or recompence the same[,]
But feare that we have not worthely received
the same[;] And consydering further also with our self
that we be[,] as all mankind is[,] mortall and born
in sinne[,] beleving nevertheles and hoping that every
chrenen creature lyving here in this transitory and
wretched woorld under God[,] dying in stedfast
and perfaict faith[,] endevoring and exercising himself
to execute in his lief tyme if he have leasyr such
good dedes and charitable workes as scripture demandeth[2][,]
and as may be to the honour and pleasyr of God[,]

[FOLIO 2]

is ordeyned by Christes passion to be saved and to atteyn

eternall lief[,] of which nombre we verily trust by

his grace to be oon. And that every creature the

more high that he is in estate honour & authorite

in this woorld[,] the more he is bound to love serve

and thank God and the more diligently to endevor

himself to do good and charitable workes to the

lawde honour and praise of almighty God and the

profit of his sowle. We also, calling to our

remembraunce the dignite estate honour rule & gouvernance

that almighty God hath called us unto in this woorld

and that neither we[,] nor any other creature mortall[,]

knowith the tyme place whenne ne where it

shall pleas almighty God to call him out of this

transitory woorld[,] willing therefor and minding with Godes

grace[,] before our passage out of the same[,] to dispose and ordre

our Latter mynd Will and Testament in that sort as

we trust it shalbe acceptable to Almighty God[,] our

only Savyour Jesus Christ[,] and the hole company of

Heaven[,] and the due satisfaction of all godly brethren

[FOLIO 3]

in erth have therefore[,] nowe being of hole and perfaict
mynde[,] adhering holy to the right faith of Christ
and his doctrine, repenting also our old and detestable
lief[,] and being in perfaict will and mynde by his grace
never to return to the same nor such like[,] and minding
by Goddes grace never to vary therefro as long as
any remembraunce breth or inward knowledge doth
or may remayn within this mortal body, Moost
humbly and hartly do commend and bequeyth our soull
to Almighty God[,] who in personne of the sonne
redeamed the same with his moost precious body and
blood in tyme of his passion[,] And[,] for our better
remembraunce thereof[,] hath left here with us in his
church militant the consecration and administration
of his precious body and blood to our no little consolation
and comfort, if we as thankfully accept the same
as he Lovingly and undeserved on mannes behalf hath
ordeyned it for our only benefite and not his. / Also
we do instantly requyre and desyre the blessed Virgin
Mary his mother with all the holy company of heaven
contynually to pray for us and with us whiles we lyve
in this woorld and in the tyme of passing out of

[FOLIO 4]

the same, that we may the³ soner atteyn everlasting lief
after our departure out of this transitory lief. Which
we do both hope and clayme by Christes passion
and woord[;] And as for my body which whenne
the soul is departed shall thenne remayn but as a
cadaver and so return to the vile mater it was
made of[,] wer it not for the rowme⁴ and dignitye
which God hath called us unto[,] and that we woold
not be noted an Infringer of honest worldly politics
and custumes whenne they be not contrary to Godes
Lawes[,] we woold be content to have it buryed
in any place accustumed for chrenen folkes wer it never
so vile ffor it is but ashes and to ashes it shal
again[.] Nevertheles[,] bicaus we woold be lothe in
the reputation of the people to do iniurye to the
dignite which we unworthely ar callid unto[,] We
ar content and also[,] by these presentes our last Will and
Testament[,] do will and ordeyn that our body be buryed
and ienterred in the Quere of our College of Windesor
midway betwen the stattes and the high Aultaur[,]
and there to be made and sett assone[ ]as convenently

[FOLIO 5]

may be doon after our deceasse by our Executours at
our costes and charges[,] if it be not done by us in our
lief tyme[,] an honorable tombe for our bones to rest in[,]
which is well onward and almoost made therfor
alredye[,] with a fayre grate about it[,] in which we
will also that the bones and body of our true and
Loving Wief Quene Jane be putt also[,] And that
there be provided ordeyned made and sett at the
costes and charges of us or of our executours if it be
not done in our lyf[,] a convenent aulter honorably
prepared[,] and apparailled with all maner of thinges
requisite and necessary for dayly masses there
to be sayd perpetuelly while the woorld shal
endure[;] Also we will that the Tombes and
Aultars of King Henry the VIt and also of King
Edward the fourth our great uncle and grauntfather
be made more princely in the same place where
they now be at our charges, And also will and
specially desyre and requyre that where and whensoever
it shall pleas God to call us out of the woorld
transitory to his infinite mercy and grace[,] be it
beyonde the See or in any other place without our
Realme of Englande or within the same[,] that our
Executours[,] assone[ ]as convenently they may[,] shall cause

[FOLIO 6]

all divine service accustumed for dead folkes[5] to be celebrate

for us in the nixt and moost propre place where it

shall fortune us to depart out of this transitory

lief[,] And over that we will that whensoever

or wheresoever it shall pleas God to call us out

of this transitory lief to his infinite mercy and grace[,]

be it within this realme or without[,] that our executours[,]

in as goodly brief and convenient hast as they reasonably

canne or may[,] ordeyn prepare and cause our body to

be removed conveyed and brought in to the sayde

College of Windesor[,] and the service of Placebo and

Dirige with a sermon and Masse on the morowe

at our costes and charges devoutely to be don observed

and solemply kept there to be buryed and enterred

in the place appoincted for our sayd Tombe to be

made for the same entent[,] And all this to be doon

in as devout wise as canne or may be doon[,] And

we will and charge our executours that they

dispose and gyve in almes to the moost poore and

nedy people that may be found [(]commyn beggars

as moch as may be avoyded[)] in as short space as

possibly they may after our departure out of this

transitory lief[,] oon thousand markes of laufull money

[FOLIO 7]

of Englande[,] part in the same place and thereaboutes[,]

where it shall pleas Almighty God to call us

to his mercy[,] part by the waye[,] and part in the

same place of our buryall after their discretions[,]

and to move the poore people that shall have our

almez to pray hartly unto God for remission of

our offenses and the wealth of our soull[.]

Also we woll that with as convenient spede as

may be doon after our departure out of this woorld[,]

if it be not doon in our lief[,] that the Deane and

Channons of our free Chaple of Sainct George

within our Castle of Windesor[,] shall have manours

Landes tenementes and spirituall promotiones to the yerely

value of six hundred poundes over all charges, made

sure to them to them⁶ and their successours for ever[,]

upon these conditions hereafter ensuryng[;] And for the

due and full accomplishement and parformaunce

of all other thinges conteyned with the same in the

forme of an Indenture signed with our own hand[,]

which shalbe passed by waye of couvenant for that

purpose betwen the said Deane and Cannons and

our executours[,] if it passe not between us

and the said Deane and Cannons ˄ in our lief[,] that is to saye[,] the sayd

Deane and Cannons⁷ ˄ and theyr

Successours for ever shall fynd twoo priestes

to say masses at the said Aulter to be made

[FOLIO 8]

where we have before appoincted our tombe to be made
and stand[,] And also after our deceasse kepe yerely
foure solempne obites for us within the sayd College
of Wyndesour[,] and at every of the same obites to
cause a solempne sermon to be made[;] And also at
every[8] of the sayd obites to give to poore people in
almez tenne poundes[;] And also to gyve for ever yerly
to thirtene poor men which shalbe called poore
knightes to every of them twelf pens every daye[,] and
ones in the yere yerely for ever a long gowne of white
cloth, with the garter upon the brest embrodered
with a shelde and crosse of Sainte George
within the garter and a mantel of red cloth[,] and to
such one of the sayd thirtene poore knightes as shalbe
appoincted to be hed and gouvernour of them iii *l.* vi *s.* viii *d.*
yerely forever over and besides the sayd twelf pennes
by the daye[;] And also to cause every Sonday in the
yere for ever a sermon to be made for ever at Windesor
aforsayde as in the sayd Indenture and couvenuant
shalbe more fully and particulerly expressed. Willing
charging and requyring our sonne Prince Edward[,]
all our Executours and counsaillours which shalbe
named hereafter[,] and all other our heyres and
Successours which shalbe kinges of this realme as
they will aunswer before almighty God at the dredfull

[FOLIO 9]

Daye of Judgment[,] that they and every of them do see
that the sayd Indenture and assurance to be made
betwen us and the sayd Deane and Channons[,] or
betwen them and our executours and all thinges therin
conteyned may be duely put in execution and observed
and kept forever perpetuelly according to this our
Last Will and Testament. And as concerning
the ordre and disposition of th[']imperial croune of
this Realme of England and Irland with our title
of Fraunce and all dignityes honours preeminences prerogatives authorityes and jurisdictions to the same
annexed or belonging[,] and for the sure establishement
of the succession of the same[.] And also for a full
and plain gift disposition assignement declaration
limitation and appoinctement with what conditions our
doughters Mary and Elizabeth shall severally
have hold and enioye the sayd imperial Crowne
and other the premisses after our deceasse and
for default[9] of issue and heyres of the severall
bodyes of us and of our sonne prince Edward
Laufully begotten and his heyres. And also for a
full gift disposition assignement declaration limitation
and appoinctement to whom[,] and of what estate[,]
and in what maner forms and condition the sayde
Imperial Crowne and other the premisses shall remayn

[FOLIO 10]

and cum after our deceasse and for[10] default of Issue

and heyres of the several bodyes of us and of our

sayd sonne prince Edwarde and of our sayd doughters

Mary and Elizabeth Laufully begotten[,] We

by these presentes do make and declare our Last Will

and Testament concerning the said Imperial Crowne

and all other the premisses in maner and forme

folowing[;] That is to saye we will be these presentes[,]

that imedyately after our departure out of this present

lief[,] Our sayd sonne Edward shall have and

enioye the sayd imperial crowne and Realm of

Englande and Irlande[,] our title to Fraunce[,] with all

dignityes honours and preeminences, prerogatives authorites

and jurisdictions Landes and possessions to the

same annexed or belonging to him and his heyres

of his body Laufully begotten[;] And for default of such

Issue of our sayde sonne prince Edwards bodye

Laufully begotten[,] we will the sayd imperiall crown

and other the premisses[,] after our two deceasses,

shall holly remayn and cum to the heyres of our

body Laufully begotten of the body of our entierly

beloved wief Quene Katheryn[11] that now is or of

any other our Lawfull Wief that we shall herafter

mary[;] And for lack of such Issue and

[FOLIO 11]

heyres[,] we will also that after our deceasse[,] and for

default of heyres of the several bodyes of us and

of our said sonne prince Edward Laufully begotten[,]

the said[12] imperial Crown and all other the premisses

shall holly remayn and cum to our sayd doughter

Mary ˄ and the heires of her body[13] ˄ Laufully begotten[,] upon condition that

our sayd doughter Mary after our deceasse

shall not mary ne take any personne to her husband

without the assent and consent of the pryvey

consaillours and others appoincted by us to to be of counsail with[14] ˄ our
deerest

sonne prince Edwarde aforsayd to be of counsail[,] or of the

moost part of them[,] or the moost part of such as shall

thene be alyve[,] therunto[,] before the sayd mariage[,]

had in writting sealed with their seales. All which

condition we declare limite appoinct and will by

these presentes shalbe knitt and invested to the sayd

estate of our sayd doughter Mary in the sayde

Imperial crown and other the premisses. And if

it fortune our sayd doughter Mary to dye without

issue of her body Laufully begotten[,] we will[,] that

after our deceasse, and for default of Issue of

the severall bodyes of us, and of our sayd sonne prince

Edwarde Laufully begotten and of our doughter

Mary[,] the sayd imperial crown and other the premisses

[FOLIO 12]

shall holly remayn and cum to our sayd doughter Elizabeth[,]
and to the heyres of her body Laufully begotten[,] upon
condition[15] that our sayd doughter Elizabeth after our
deceasse shall not marry nor take any personne to her
husbande without the assent and consent of[16] the privey
Counsaillours and others appoincted by us to be of counsaill
with our sayd deerest sonne prince Edwarde[,] or the moost
part of them[,] or the moost part of such of them as
shalbe thenne on lyve[,] therunto[,] before the same mariage
had in writting sealed with their seales[,] which
condition we declare limitt appoinct and will be these
presentes, shalbe to the sayd estate of our sayd doughter
Elizabeth in the sayd imperial Crown and other
the premisses knitt and invested. And if it shall
fortune our sayd doughter Elizabeth to dye without
Issue of her body Laufully begotten[,] we will that after
our deceasse, and for default of issue of the
severall bodyes of us, and of our sayd sonne prince
Edwarde and of our sayd doughters Mary and
Elizabeth[,] Laufully begotten. We will that[17] the
sayd imperial crown and other the premisses after
our deceasse and for default of th[']issue of the
several bodyes of us[,] and of our sayd sonne prince
Edwarde[,] and of our sayd doughters Mary &

[FOLIO 13]

Elizabeth Laufully begotten[,] shall holly remayn and cum

to the heyres of the body of the Lady Fraunces,

our Niepce[,] eldest doughter to our late suster the

French Quene Laufully begotten[,] and for default

of such Issue of the body of the sayd Lady

Fraunces[,] we will that the sayd imperial

Crown and other the premisses after our deceasse

and for default of issue of the several bodys

of us[,] and of our sonne prince Edward, and

of our doughters Mary and Elizabeth[,] and

of the Lady Fraunces Laufully begotten[,] shall

holly remayn and cum to the heyres of the bodye

of the Lady Elyanore our niepce[,] second doughter

to our sayd Late Sister the french Quene

Laufully begotten[;] And if it happen the sayd

Lady Elyanore to dye without issue of her body

Laufully begotten[,] we will that after our deceasse[,]

and for default of issue of the several bodys

of us[,] and of our sayd sonne prince Edwarde[,]

and of our said doughters Mary and Elizabeth[,]

and of the sayd Lady Fraunces[,] and of the sayd

Lady Elyanore Laufully begotten[,] the sayd imperial

Crown and other the premisses shall holly remayn

[FOLIO 14]

and cum to the next rightfull heyres.

Also we will that if our sayd doughter Mary do
mary without the consent and agreement of the pryvey
Counsaillours and others appointed by us to be of counsail
to our sayd sonne prince Edwarde or the moost part
of them[,] or the moost part of such of them as shall
thenne be alyve[,] therunto[,] before the sayd mariage
had in writting sealed with their seales as is aforsaid[,]
that thenne and from thensforth for lack of heyres
of the several bodyes of us[,] and of our said sonne
prince Edwarde Laufully begotten[,] the sayde
imperial crown and other the premisses shall holly
remayn be and cum to our sayd doughter Elizabeth
and to the heyres of her body Laufully begotten in
such maner and forme as though our sayd doughter
Mary wer thenne dead without any yssue of the
body of our sayd doughter Mary Laufully begotten[,]
Any thing conteyned in this our will[,] or in any act
of parliament or statute to the contrary in any
wise notwithstanding[,] And in cace our said doughter
the Lady Mary do kepe[18] and parforme the sayd
condition expressed declared and limited to her
estate in the sayd imperial Crown and other

[FOLIO 15]

the premisses by this our Last Will declared[;] And
that our sayd doughter Elizabeth for her part
do not kepe and parforme the sayd condition declared
and limited by this our Last Will to the estate
of the sayd Lady Elizabeth[19] in the said imperial
crown of this realme of England and Irlande
and other the premisses[,] we will that thenne and
from thensforth after our deceas[,] and for lack of
heyres of the several bodyes of us[,] and of our sayd
sonne prince Edwarde[,] and of our said doughter
Mary Laufully begotten, the said imperiall crown
and other the premisses shall holly remayn &
cum to the next heyres Laufully begotten of the body
of the sayd Lady Fraunces[,] in such maner and forme
as though the sayd Lady Elizabeth wer then
dead without any heyres of her body Laufully begotten[;]
Any thing conteyned in this will, or in any act or
statute to the contrary notwithstanding[:] The
remaindres over for lack of issue of the sayde
Lady Fraunces Laufully begotten[,] to be and contynue
to such personnes like remaindres and estates as is
before Limited and Declared[.]
Also we being now at this tyme[,] thankes be to almighty
God[,] of parfaict memory[,] do constitute and ordeyn
these personnages folowing our executours & parformers

[FOLIO 16]

of this our Last Will and Testament[,] Willing commanding
and praing them to take upon them th[']occupation and
parformance of this same as executours[,] That is to
saye; Th[']Archebishop of Canterbury, The Lord
Wriothesley Chancelour of Englande, The Lord
St. John great M[aste]r of our house[,] Th'erle of Hertford,
great Chambrelain of Englande, The lord Russel
lord privey Seale, The Visconte Lisle high Admiral
of Englande, The bishop Tunstall of Duresme,
Sir Anthony Brown Knight m[aste]r of our hors[,] Sir
Edward Montagu Knight chief Juge of the comyn
Place[,] Iustice Bromley[,] Sir Edward North Knight
chauncelour of th[']augmentations[,] Sir William Paget Knight our
Chief Secretary[,] Sir Anthony Denny[,] Sir William Harbard
Knightes chief gentlemen of our privey chamber, Sir
Edward Wootton Knight and Mr. Doctor Wootton his
brother[.] and all these, we woll to be our executours
and counsaillours of the pryvey Counsail with our said
sonne prince Edwarde, in all maters concerning both
his private affayres and publicq affayres of the
Realme[,] Willing and charging them and every of
them[,] as they must and shall aunswer at the Day
of Judgement[,] truely and fully to see this my
Last Will performed in all thingz with as moch spede
and diligence as may be and that noon of them

[FOLIO 17]

presume to medle with any of our treasyr or to do any thing

appoincted by our sayd will alone[,] onles the moost

part of the hole nombre of their coexecutours do

consent and by writting agree to the same[.] And

will that our said executours or the moost part of

them may Laufully do what they shall think

moost convenient for th[']execution of this our Will

without being troubled by our sayd sonne or any others

for the same[.] Willing further by this our

Last Will and testament that Sir Edmund Peckham[20][,]

our trusty servaunt and yet coserar of our house[,]

shalbe Treasorer, and have the receipt and laying

out of all such treaser and money as shalbe defrayed

by our executors for the performaunce of this our Last

Will straictly chargyng and comaunding the sayd

Sir Edmunde that he pay no great somme of money

but he have furst the handes of our said executours

or of the moost part of them for his discharge

touching the same[,] Charging him further upon his

allegeaunce to make a true accompt of all such

sommes as shalbe delivered to his handz for this

purpose[.] And sithens we have now

named and constituted our executours[,] we woll

and charge them that furst and above all thinges[,]

[FOLIO 18]

as they will aunswer before God and as we putt our

singuler trust and confidence in them[,] that they cause

all our due debtes that can be reasounably shewed

and proved before them[,] to be truely contented and payd

assone as they conueniently can or may after our deceas

without lenger delaye[.] And that they do execute

these poinctes furst[:] That is to say, the payment of

our debtes with redres of injuries[,] if any such can be

duely proved though to us they be unknown[,]

before any other part of this our Will and testament,

our buryall exequyes and funeralles only excepted.

Furthermore we woll that all such grauntes and giftes

as we have made gyven or promised to any[,] which

be not yet perfaicted under our Signe or any our

seales as they ought to be[,] and all such[ ]recompenses

for exchaunges Sales or any other thing or thinges,

as ought to have been made by us[,] and be not yet

accomplished[,] shalbe perfaicted in every point towardes

all maner of men for discharge of our conscience[,]

charging our executours and all the rest of our counsaillors

to see the same done performed finished and accomplished

in every poinct[,] forseing that the sayd giftz grauntes

promises and recompenses shall appear to our sayd executours

or the moost part of them to have been graunted made

as they will answere before god and as we putt our
singuler trust and confidence in them that they cause
all our due dettes that can be reasonablie shewed
and proved before them to be truely contented and payed
as sone as they convenientlie can or may after our decease
withowt lengor delaye And that they do performe
theise pointes first That is to say the paymentes of
our dettes to widowes of Injuries if any suche can be
duely proved thoughe to be they be contynued
before any other parte of this our wille and testament
our buryall expenses and funeralle only excepted

Furthermore we woll that all suche grauntes and giftes
as we have made gyven or promised to any whiche
be not yet perfourmed under our Signe or any our
sealles as they ought to be and all suche recompenses
for exchaunges Sales or any suche thing or thinges
as ought to have been made by us and be not yet
accomplisshed shalbe perfourmed in every point towardes
all maner of men for discharge of our conscience
chargynge our executours and all the rest of our counsaillors
to see the same done performed finisshed and accomplisshed
in every poynt forseynge that the said giftes grauntes
promiss and recompence shall appear to our said executours
or the most part of them to have been grauntid made

Mary Tudor, painted in 1544 by the artist known as Master John. This beautiful portrait shows Henry VIII's eldest daughter at the age of twenty-seven. With features very similar to her father's —the same auburn hair and small mouth—she appears plain to the modern eye, although she is gloriously attired. The portrait names her as "Ladi Mari," as she had been stripped of the title "Princess" by the Act of Succession in 1536. © *National Portrait Gallery, London, UK.*

Edward VI, painted by William Scrots in 1547. This gorgeous picture shows the new king standing in almost precisely the same stance as Henry VIII in the Whitehall Mural, and the viewer is invited to draw visual parallels: Edward is to be seen as a chip off the old block, the reincarnation of the old king. Note the richness of the velvet and ermine worn by Edward, and also the padded doublet, designed to make him look more manly than this boy-king actually was. *Royal Collection Trust © Her Majesty Queen Elizabeth II, 2015/Bridgeman Images.*

Mary Stuart, Queen of Scots, painted by François Clouet. This portrait shows the fabled beauty of Mary Stuart (1542–87), who became Queen of Scotland at just eight days old. It was probably painted shortly before, or during, Mary's marriage to the Dauphin of France (1558–60), who became King Francis II of France in 1559. Despite being the granddaughter of Henry VIII's sister, Margaret, she was excluded from the English line of succession by Henry's last will and testament. Nevertheless, her son, King James VI of Scotland—whose father (Henry Stuart, Lord Darnley) was also a grandchild of Margaret Tudor, by a different marriage—would inherit the English throne from Henry's daughter, Elizabeth, in 1603. © *Czartoryski Museum, Krakow, Poland/Bridgeman Images.*

RIGHT: Edward Seymour (1500–52), Earl of Hertford, depicted by Hans Holbein. This portrait, painted when Hertford was Great Chamberlain of England, allows the viewer to see the whites of the eyes of the man who would become Duke of Somerset and Lord Protector of England. © *The Trustees of the Weston Park Foundation, UK/Bridgeman Images.*

LEFT: This anxious-looking man, dressed in very rich blacks and sporting a fashionable sugarloaf beard, is Sir William Paget (1506–63), formerly Chief Secretary to Henry VIII and, at the time of this picture, co-architect of England's protectorate with Edward Seymour. He carries a roll of paper in honor of his position. The portrait is attributed to an unknown Flemish artist and dated to 1549. © *National Portrait Gallery, London, UK.*

John Dudley, Viscount Lisle, painted posthumously *c*.1600. Dudley (1504–54) was made Lord High Admiral of England under Henry VIII. He was created Earl of Warwick and, later, Duke of Northumberland under Edward VI. Dudley was one of the men in whom Henry VIII placed his faith in his last will and testament, and he became, with Edward Seymour, a leading figure of government under Edward VI. His attempt to install his daughter-in-law, Lady Jane Grey, on the throne would prove his undoing. *Knole Park, Kent, UK/National Trust Photographic Library.*

The Lady Elizabeth—the future Elizabeth I—in a portrait attributed to William Scrots. This painting shows Elizabeth in around 1546, a year before Henry died. She is dressed in gorgeously rich attire, and is wearing the round English headdress that her mother made fashionable, and which shows off her auburn hair. The picture also displays her learning and piety—the small book in her hands is probably the New Testament, while the large book behind her is likely to be the Old Testament. The portrait is first recorded in the collection of her half brother, Edward VI, where it is described as "the picture of the Ladye Elizabeth her grace with a booke in her hande her gowne like crymsen clothe." *Royal Collection Trust © Her Majesty Queen Elizabeth II, 2015/Bridgeman Images.*

LEFT: Ceiling of the quire of St George's Chapel, at Windsor Castle. Under this intricate fan-vaulted ceiling, which was added to the chapel by Henry VII, King Henry VIII is buried, beneath the floor of the south quire aisle. His final resting place is marked by a simple black marble slab, inscribed in gold letters: "In a vault beneath this marble slab are deposited the remains of Jane Seymour, Queen of King Henry VIII 1537. King Henry VIII 1547. King Charles I 1648. And an infant child of Queen Anne. Memorial placed by William IV 1837." It is far from the elaborate tomb Henry VIII had planned in his will; yet it does demonstrate that, at the end, the king chose to be buried with the one wife who had ensured the accomplishment of the "chief goal" of his life and will: a smooth succession. *Steve Vidler/Alamy Stock Photo.*

RIGHT: A portrait of King Charles I, by Daniel Mytens (1631). The Stuart monarch is here depicted with the Tudor imperial crown—the same crown that Henry VIII's inventory describes as "the King's Crown of gold, garnished with 6 balas, 5 sapphires, 5 pointed diamonds . . ." *Ann Ronan Pictures/Print Collector/Getty Images.*

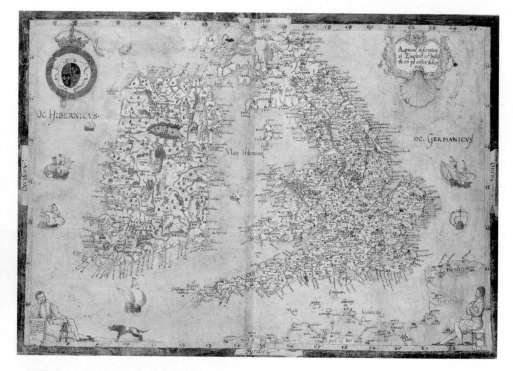

A Tudor conception of what Henry's will, in folio 9, describes as "this Realme of England and Irland," here mapped out (*c.*1564) by Laurence Nowell. This beautiful map was commissioned by Sir William Cecil, who served the Duke of Somerset in the late 1540s as a secretary and who rose to become Elizabeth I's durable chief minister. *British Library Board/Topfoto.*

Folios 18 and 19 of Henry VIII's last will and testament, as preserved in the National Archives, Kew. It is these pages that include the notorious "unfulfilled gifts" clause, the subject of considerable historical controversy. *The National Archives.*

[FOLIO 19]

accorded or promised by us or in any maner wise.
Further[,] according to the Lawes of Almighty God and
for the fatherly love which we beare to our sonne
Prince Edwarde and to this our Realme[,] We
declare him according to iustice equite and conscience
to be our Laufull heyre and do gyve and bequeith
unto him the Succession of our Realmes of
England and Irlande[,] with our title of Fraunce &
all our dominions both on thisside the sees and
beyond (a convenient portion for our Will & testament
to be reserved)[.] Also we give unto him all
our plate stuff of household Artillery Ordenaunce
Munitions ships cabettes[21] and all other thinges &
implementz to them belonging[,] and money also and
Jewelz, saving such portions as shall satisfye
this our Last Will and Testament, Charging
and commanding him on peyn of our curse[,] seing
he hath so loving a father of us and that our
chief labour and study in this world is to
establishe him in the Crown Imperial of this
Realme[22] after our deceasse in such sort as may
be pleasing to God[,] and to the wealth of this realme,
and to his own honour and quyet, that he be
ordred and ruled both in his mariage and also

[FOLIO 20]

in ordering of th[']affaires of the Realme as wel outward
as inwarde[,] and also in all his oun private affayres[,]
and in gyving of offices of charge by th[']advise &
counsail of our right entierly beloved Counsaillours[,]
th[']archebishop²³ of Cantorbury, the lord Wriothesley
Chancelour of England, The lord St. John great
M[aste]r of our house, The Lord Russel Lord privey Seale,
Th'erle of Hertford great Chambrelain of Englande,
The Visconte Lisle high Admiral of England
The Bishop of Duresme Tunstall, Sir Anthonye
Broun M[aste]r of our Horse[,] Sir William Paget our chiefe
Secretarye, Sir Anthony Denny[,] Sir William Herberd
Iustices Montague and Bromley[,] Sir Edward Wootton
and M[aste]r Doctor Wootton and Sir Edward North[,]
Whom we ordeyn name and appoinct[,] and by these presentes
signed with our hand do make and constitute of privey ˄ counsail ˄
with our sayd sonne, and woll that they have the
gouvernement of our moost deere sonne prince Edward
and of all our Realmes dominions and Subjectz[,] and of
all th[']affayres publicq and private until he shall
have fully accompleted the eightenth year of his age[.]
And for bicaus²⁴ the variete and nombre of thinges
affayres and materes ar and may be such as we[,]
not knowing the certainty of them before[,] cannot
conveniently prescribe a certain order or Rule

[FOLIO 21]

unto our forsayd counsaillours for their behavoiurs and
procedinges in this charge[,] which we have now &
do appoinct unto them about our sayd sonne[,] during
the tyme of his minorite aforesayde, We therefor[,]
for the sp[ec]iall trust and confidence which we
have in them[,] woll[,] and by these presentes do give
and graunt²⁵[,] full powre and authorite unto our
sayd Counsaillours that they all[,] or the moost
part of them[,] being assembled togidres in counsaill[,]
or if any of them fortune to dye the more part
of them which shalbe for the tyme lyving[,] being
assembled in Counsaill togidres, shall and may
make devise and ordeyn what thinges soever
they or the more part of them as forsayd shall[,]
during the minorite aforsayde of our said sonne
think meet necessary or convenient for the benifit
honour and suretye or the weale profet or²⁶
commodytye of our sayd sonne his Realms
dominions or Subgectz, or discharge of ₍our₎ conscience[,]
And the same thinges devised made or ordeyned
by them or the more part of them[,] as aforsayd[,]
shall and may Laufully do execute and accomplishe,
or cause to be done executed and accomplished
by their discretions[,] or the discretions of the

[FOLIO 22]

more part of them[,] as aforsayde, In as large and ample
maner as if we had or did expresse unto them by
a more sp[e]call commission under our great Seale
of Englande, every particuler cause that may chaunce
or occurre during the tyme of our sonnes sayde
minorite[,] and the self same maner of proceding
which they shall for the tyme think meet to use
and folowe[;] Willing and charging our sayd
sonne[,] and all others which shall hereafter be
Counsaillours to our sayd sonne[,] that they never
charge molest trouble nor disquyet our forsayde
Counsaillours[,] nor any of them[,] for the devising or
doing[,] nor any other personne for the doing of that they
shall devise[,] or the more part of them devise or
do assembled as aforesaid; And we do
charge expressely the same our entierly beloved
Counsaillours and executours[,] that they shall take
upon them the rule and charge of our sayd sonne
and heyre in all his causes and affayres[,] and of
the hole Realme[,] doing nevertheles all thinges
as under him and in his name[,] until our sayde
sonne and heyre shalbe bestowed and maryed
by their advise[,] and that the eightenth yere be
expyred[;] Willing and desyring furthermore
our forsayd trusty Counsaillours[,] and then all our

[FOLIO 23]

trusty and assured servauntz[,] and thirdly all other our
Loving Subgectz to ayde and assist our fornamed
Counsaillours in th[']execution of the premisses during
the forsayd tyme[,] Not doubting but they will
in all thinges deale so truely and uprightly as
they shall have cause to think them well chosen
for the charge committed unto them[;] Straictly
charging our sayd counsaillours and executours[,]
and in Goddes name we exhort them, that for the
singuler trust and special confidence which
we have and ever had in them[,] to have a due
and diligent eye[,] perfaict zeale[,] love and affection
to the honour[,] suretye[,] estate and dignitye of our
sayd sonne[,] and the good state and prosperite
of this our Realme[,] And that[,] all delayes sett
a part[,] they will ayd and assiste our sayd
Counsaillours and executours to the performaunce
of this our present Testament and Last Will
in every part as they will aunswer before God
at the Daye of judgement[,] Cum venerit Iudicare
vivos et mortuos[.]
And furthermore for the sp[ec]iall trust and confidence
which we have in the Erles of Arundel and
Essex that nowe be[,] Sir Thomas Cheney Knight[,]
Treasorer of our household[,] Sir John Gage Knight[,]

[FOLIO 24]

Comptroller of our household[,] Sir Anthony Wingfeld
Knight our Vichambrelayn[,] Sir William Petre Knight[,]
oon of our twoo principall Secretarys[,] Sir Richard
Riche Knight[,] Sir John Baker Knight[,] Sir Rafe
Sadleyr Knight[,] Sir Thomas Seymour Knight,
Sir Richard Southwell and Sir Edmund Peckham
Knightes[,] they and every of them shalbe of counsail
for the ayding and assisting of the fornamed
Counsaillours and our executours, whenne they or
any of them shalbe called by our sayd executours
or the more part of the same[.]
Item, we bequethe to our doughters Mary and
Elizabeth[']s mariages[,] they being maried to any outward
potentate by th[']advise of the forsayd Counsaillours[,]
if we bestowe them not in our lief tyme, ten thousand poundz
in money plate Iewelz and household stuff for ech
of them[,] or a Larger somme as to the discretion of
our executours or the more part of them shalbe
thought convenient[,] Willing them on my blessing
to be ordered aswel in mariage as in all other
Laufull thinges by th[']advise of our forsayde
Counsaillours, and in cace they will not[,] thenne
the somme to be minished at the Counsaillours[']
discretion;

[FOLIO 25]

Further our Will is that[,] from the furst howre of
our death until such tyme as the sayde
Counsaillours canne provide either of them or bothe
of sum honorable mariages[,] they shall have
eche of them thre thousand poundes[,] ultra reprisas[,]
to lyve on[,] willing and charging the forsayde
Counsaillours to Limite and appoinct to either of them
such sage officers and ministers for ordering
thereof[,] as it may be employed both to our honour
and theirs.
And for the great love obedyence chastnes of lief
and wisedom[,] being in our fornamed Wief and Quene[,]
We bequeth unto her for her proper use, and as
it shall pleas her to ordre it[,] thre thousand poundes
in plate Iewelz and Stuff of household[,] besides
such apparail as it shall pleas her to take
of such as she hath allredy[;] And further we
gyve unto her one thousand poundes in money[,] with the
enioying of her dower and Ioynter accordinge
to our graunt by Act of Parliament[.]
Furthermore for the kindnes and good service that
our sayd executours have shewed unto us[,] we
gyve and bequethe unto eche of them such somes

[FOLIO 26]

of money or the value of the same as hereafter ensuith[;]

Firste, to Th[']Archebishop of Cantorbury—V C [500][27] m[ar]ks

To the lord Wriothesley—V C [500] li   [28] To the lord

Seint John—V C [500] li   To the Lord Russell

V C [500][29] li   To Th[']erle of Hertford—V C [500] li

To the Visconte Lisle—V C [500] li   To the bishop

of Duresme—CCC [300] li   To Sir Anthonye

Broun—CCC [300] li   To Sir William Paget CCC [300] li

To Sir Anthony Denny—CCC [300] li   To Sir

William Herbert—CCC [300] li   To Iustice

Montague—CCC [300] li   To Iustice Bromley—

CCC [300] li   To Sir Edward North—CCC [300] li

To Sir Edward Wootton—CCC [300] li   To Mr

Doctor Wootton—CCC [300] li   . Also for

the sp[ec]iall love and favour that we bear to our trusty

Counsaillours and other our sayd servaunts herafter folowing[,]

we gyve and bequeyth unto them such sommes of

money or the value thereof[,] as it totted upon their hedes[;]

First to th'erle of Essex—CC [200] li   To Sir

Thomas Cheney—CC [200] li   To the lord

Herberd—CC [200] li   To Sir John Gage

CC [200] li   To Sir Thomas Seymour—CC [200] li

To Sir John Gates Knight—CC [200] li   To Sir

Thomas Darcy Knight—CC [200] li   To Sir Thomas

[FOLIO 27]

Speke Knight—CC [200] mkes To Sir Philip Hobby Knight CC [200] mkes

Sir Thomas Paston CC [200] mkes To Sir Maurice Barkley CC [200] mkes[30]

To Sir Rafe Sadleyr CC [200] li To Sir Thomas Carden—CC [200] li.

To Sir Peter Mewtes[31] CC [200] mkes To Edward Bellingham CC [200] mkes

To Thomas Audeley CC [200] mkes To Edmunde Harman CC [200] mkes

To John Pen C [100] mkes To Henry Nevel C [100] li To

Symbarde C [100] li To   Cooke C [100] li   To John

Osburn C [100] li   To David Vincent C [100] li   To James

Rufforth Keper of our hous here C [100] mkes To

Cecill yoman of our Robes C [100] mkes To   Sternhold

grome of our robes C [100] mkes To John Rouland page

of our Robes L [50] li   To th[']erle of Arundel

Lord Chambrelain CC [200] li   To Sir Anthony Wingfeld

Vizchambrelain CC [200] li   To Edmund Peckham CC [200] li

To Sir Richard Riche CC [200] li To Sir John Bak[er][32] [CC [200] li

To Sir Richard Southwell CC [200] li To Mr. D[octor]

Owen C [100] li To Mr. doctor Wendy C [100] li T[o]

Mr. doctor Cromer C [100] li To   Alsopp [C [100] mkes]

To Patrick   C [100] mkes To   A[lyliff C [100] mkes]

To   Ferrys C [100] mkes To Henry   [C [100] mkes]

To   Hollande C [100] mkes To the four [gentlemen]

huissers of our chambre being dayly wayters CC [200 li]

And we will also that our executours[,] or the more part

of them[,] shall gyve ordre for the payment of such

Legacyes as they shall think meet to such our

ordinary servauntes[,] as unto whom we have not

appoincted any legacye by this our present Testament[:]

[FOLIO 28]

Finally this present writting in paper we ordeyn and
make our Last Will and Testament, and will the
same to be reputed and taken to all ententes and
purposes for our good strong vaillable moost parfait
and Last Will and Testament, and do declare
all other Willes and Testamentes made at any tyme
by us to be voyd and of non effect[.] In witnes
whereof we have signed it with our hand in our
Palays of Westm[inste]r the thirty Day of Decembre
in the year of our Lord God a thousand fyve hundred
fourty and six after the computation of the church
of England, and of our reign the eight and thirty
yere being present and called to be witnesses
these personnes which have written their names
herunder.

        HENRY R.

        John Gates

George Owen   E. HARMAN

Thomas Wendye   Wyllyam Sayntbarbe

Robert Huycke

        Henry Nevell

        Richard Coke

        David Vincent

        Patrec

    W. Clerk.

[COVERING FOLIO]

(?) Confirmatus in dors(um) clavis cancellarii domini nostri [regii]
Edwardi sexti de anno regni sui [primo]

The final folio of Henry VIII's last will and testament. This last page gives the date of the will's creation—December 30, 1546—and is signed by Henry VIII (his dry stamp) and by his ten witnesses as well as his clerk, William Clerk. Contrary to suggestions that the witnesses may have signed a blank sheet into which the concluding text of the will was squeezed, the final page is as consistently spaced as the other folios and the signatures follow immediately underneath. *The National Archives.*

APPENDIX II

Council Personnel

THE EXECUTORS AND THE REGENCY COUNCIL

The sixteen executors and regency councillors named by Henry VIII in his last will and testament are as follows:

THOMAS CRANMER, *Archbishop of Canterbury**

THOMAS WRIOTHESLEY, *Lord Chancellor of England* (later Earl of Southampton)*

WILLIAM PAULET, LORD ST. JOHN, *Great Master of the King's Household and President of the Privy Council* (later Earl of Wiltshire and Marquess of Winchester)*

JOHN, LORD RUSSELL, *the Lord Privy Seal* (later Earl of Bedford)*

EDWARD SEYMOUR, EARL OF HERTFORD, *Great Chamberlain of England** *(later Duke of Somerset and Lord Protector)*

JOHN DUDLEY, VISCOUNT LISLE, *High Admiral of England* (later Earl of Warwick and Duke of Northumberland)*

CUTHBERT TUNSTAL, *Bishop of Durham**

SIR ANTHONY BROWNE, *Master of the King's Horse**

SIR WILLIAM PAGET, *"our Chief Secretary"**

DR. NICHOLAS WOTTON, *Dean of Canterbury and York**

SIR ANTHONY DENNY, *one of the Chief Gentlemen of the King's Privy Chamber*

SIR WILLIAM HERBERT, *also one of the Chief Gentlemen of the King's Privy Chamber*

SIR EDWARD NORTH, *Chancellor of the Court of Augmentations*

SIR EDWARD MONTAGU, *Chief Justice of the Commons Pleas*

SIR THOMAS BROMLEY, *a puisne justice of the King's Bench*

SIR EDWARD WOTTON, *Treasurer at Calais**

* Denotes members of Henry VIII's Privy Council on December 26, 1546.

THE ASSISTANTS

Those named "for the aiding and assisting of the forenamed councillors and executors" are:

HENRY FITZALAN, EARL OF ARUNDEL, *Lord Chamberlain of the Household**

WILLIAM PARR, EARL OF ESSEX* (later Marquess of Northampton)

SIR THOMAS CHENEY, *Treasurer of the Household**

SIR JOHN GAGE, *Comptroller of the Household**

SIR ANTHONY WINGFIELD, *Vice-Chamberlain**

SIR WILLIAM PETRE, *one of the King's two principal secretaries**

SIR RICHARD RICH*

SIR JOHN BAKER, *Chancellor of the Tenths and First Fruits**

SIR RALPH SADLER*

SIR THOMAS SEYMOUR**

SIR RICHARD SOUTHWELL

SIR EDMUND PECKHAM

> * Denotes members of Henry VIII's Privy Council on December 26, 1546.
> ** Sir Thomas Seymour was made a member of the Privy Council on January 23, 1547.

HENRY VIII'S PRIVY COUNCIL

Those who attended at least one meeting of Henry's Privy Council in 1546, and who therefore can be said to have been Henry VIII's Privy Councillors, were as follows, minuted in this order:

THOMAS CRANMER, *Archbishop of Canterbury*

THOMAS WRIOTHESLEY, *Lord Chancellor of England*

WILLIAM PAULET, LORD ST. JOHN, *Great Master of the King's Household and President of the Privy Council*

JOHN, LORD RUSSELL, *Lord Privy Seal*

EDWARD SEYMOUR, EARL OF HERTFORD, *Great Chamberlain of England*

JOHN DUDLEY, VISCOUNT LISLE, *High Admiral of England*

CUTHBERT TUNSTAL, *Bishop of Durham*

SIR ANTHONY BROWNE, *Master of the King's Horse*

SIR WILLIAM PAGET, *Secretary*

DR. NICHOLAS WOTTON, *Dean of Canterbury and York*

HENRY FITZALAN, EARL OF ARUNDEL, *Lord Chamberlain of the Household*

WILLIAM PARR, *Earl of Essex*

SIR THOMAS CHENEY, *Treasurer of the Household*

SIR JOHN GAGE, *Comptroller of the Household*

SIR ANTHONY WINGFIELD, *Vice-Chamberlain*

SIR WILLIAM PETRE, *Secretary*

SIR RICHARD RICH*

SIR JOHN BAKER, *Chancellor of the Exchequer and Under-Treasurer of England*

SIR RALPH SADLER, *Master of the Great Wardrobe and Chamberlain of the Court of General Surveyors*

STEPHEN GARDINER, *Bishop of Winchester*

THOMAS HOWARD, *Duke of Norfolk*

* Sir Richard Rich held no major office at this time—he was essentially a "minister without portfolio."

Thomas Thirlby, Bishop of Westminster seems—in theory—to have been a member of Henry's Privy Council, but he did not attend a single meeting in 1546. It may be, however, that the inclusion of the "Bishop of Westminster" in the records refers, instead, to Stephen Gardiner, who, along with the episcopacy of Winchester, technically, by pontifical appointment, held that of Westminster too.

Sir Thomas Seymour was made a member of the Privy Council on January 23, 1547.

APPENDIX III

Highlights from Henry VIII's Inventory

Six months after Henry VIII died, instructions were issued for an inventory to be made of his possessions. This mammoth task took eighteen months to complete. There are two huge parts of this inventory: the first part (now Society of Antiquaries MS 129 A), which is 469 folios in length, details his money, jewels, plate, ordnance and munition, ships, and possessions in his armories, stables, revels, and tents; the second part (now British Library Harley MS 1419 A and B), which is 562 folios, details the contents of the king's principal residences and wardrobes.

Beyond the 9,150 guns, cannons, or other pieces of artillery, over 2,000 pieces of tapestry and 2,028 pieces of plate are mentioned. What follows are a few items selected to illustrate the richness of the royal possessions at the time of Henry VIII's death, and the extensiveness of the estate that he bequeathed to the new King Edward VI. I have modernized the spelling and added punctuation.

In an act of scholarship almost equal in impressiveness to the original compilation, Dr. David Starkey, with the help of Philip Ward and Alasdair Hawkyard, prepared for publication a comprehensive list of Henry VIII's possessions. The full inventory of 17,813 itemized entries can be found in Starkey (ed.), *The Inventory of King Henry VIII, Vol. 1, The Transcript* (London, 1998). As a courtesy to readers wishing to consult the (original-spelling) versions in that volume, these selections are listed in order of the item numbers appearing there.

THE CROWN, "JEWELS OF GOLD," AND ADORNMENTS

[1] the King's Crown of gold, garnished with 6 balas [rose-colored spinel rubies], 5 sapphires, 5 pointed diamonds, 20 rubies, 19 pearls and one of the crosses of the same Crown garnished with a great sapphire, an emerald crascd, 4 balas and 9 pearls not all of one sort and 3 sapphires . . . Upon the left side of the same cross a fleur-de-lis set with an image of a king with a great balas whole and a less balas, a pointed diamond, two pearls, a collar with a sapphire and a crampion with a pearl and with 30 small pearls . . . next that one other cross with a coarse sapphire, 4 coarse balas, a fair little emerald, a lozenged diamond like a heart, a ruby and 9 pearls . . . next that one other fleur-de-lis set with a Saint George, two balas, a pointed diamond, three pearls, a collar with a sapphire and 25 pearls . . . next that one other cross with a large round sapphire, four balas, nine pearls, a collar with a sapphire . . . next that one other fleur-de-lis set with an image of Our Lady and her Child, two balas, a pointed diamond, three pearls and a sapphire and 25 pearls . . . next that one other cross set with two sapphires, 4 balas, nine pearls . . . next that one other fleur-de-lis set with an image of a king, 2 balas, a sapphire, a pointed diamond, three pearls and with 20 pearls . . . next that one other cross set with a coarse sapphire, 4 balas, 9 pearls and a sapphire loop . . . next that another fleur-de-lis set with an image of a king with two balas, a small pointed diamond, three pearls and

a sapphire with 22 pearls . . . on the diadem above 12 pointed diamonds some better than other, three triangle diamonds, one table diamond and 32 pearls, two in a troche [lozenge] with a cap of purple velvet lined with black satin, weighing together 98 ounces

[3] one Sceptre of gold with a dove thereupon weighing 12 ounces

[20] one clock of carnelian garnished with gold, diamonds, rubies, and pearls in the top of the cover being a boy with an arrow in his one hand and an antique shield with a diamond in it on the other hand [weighing] together 13 oz.

[21] one looking glass set in gold garnished in the one side with three sapphires, 4 rubies, one emerald and two pearls pendant and on the other side 4 sapphires and four rubies, the stele of Agathe, two little boys—one holding the king's arms in a shield and the other a pearl and 6 pearls hanging, on the other side of the body is a man on horseback, the body being a clock within crystal garnished with four diamonds and 56 rubies with 4 antique boys enamelled white, two of them bearing in their hands a shield with the king's arms and a pearl in either hand and the other two, the one hath two pearls and the other hath one pearl in their hands; the base or foot standing upon four round crystals garnished with ten rubies and 4 naked women of gold standing at every corner, one and a man in the top thereof being naked, [weighing] together 98 oz.

[223] an image of Our Lady with a Child and a ball with a lily in her hand and a crown garnished with glasses like sapphires and a balas with a vice [face] of silver and the base new made and she new gilt [weighing] 56 oz 3 quarters

[234] a book of Gospels garnished and wrought with antique work of silver and gilt, with an image of the crucifix with Mary and John [weighing] together 322 oz.

[2773] a man of diamond with a shield and a sword standing upon a dragon

[2806] two crosses of gold garnished with diamonds, rubies, sapphires and pearls

[3031] a Cross with a Crucifix, all gold, garnished with coarse emeralds and pearls

[3103] a lion of gold garnished with diverse gross stones of sundry sorts

[3218] one ring of gold being sometime Queen Katherine's signet

[3470] a great sapphire set in gold

DRESS

[3335] a black velvet cap with a brooch and 20 buttons of gold, small

[9915] a gown [a man's loose outer layer] with a square cape of crimson velvet and crimson satin all over embroidered with purls of damask gold and silver, having a rich border and guard of crimson velvet embroidered with damask gold and pearl, faced with crimson satin all over embroidered with damask gold and pearl, with a like border containing the said facing, being upon the sleeves of the same gown 26 diamonds set in buttons of gold, the same gown lined throughout with crimson satin and having a case of yellow sarsenet quilted

[9926] 12 pairs of hose of black silk knitted

[14207] a Spanish gown of purple damask lined with purple taffeta, faced with purple satin with 42 pairs of aglets of gold

[14229] a doublet of white silk and gold knit with hands, bought off Christofer Mulliner

[14275] a coat of leather, furred with lamb and faced with sables

[14287] a riding coat of black velvet with 3 narrow borders of cordants with Venice gold, wrought with knots, raised with the same gold, furred with ermine and faced with sables

FURNITURE

[9795] three cushions of rich cloth of tissue, the backside being of plain cloth of gold, round about with a narrow fringe of Venice gold and every of them having four buttons with tassels of Venice gold and purple silk . . .

[10503] a coffer covered with black velvet containing the physiognomy of King Henry the Eight cut in wood in a case of metal

[10580] a great table with the picture of the Duchess of Milan being her whole stature

[10632] a table with the picture of King Henry the Eight standing upon a mitre with three crowns having a serpent with seven heads coming out of it and having a sword in his hand wherein is written Verbum Dei [the Word of God]

[12323] a Cupboard of printed leather, standing upon the same: Our Lady saluted by Gabriel, with diverse goodly flowers and conceits of needlework within a glass

[12960] one chair of purple gold tissue having the King's Arms crowned, held by His Grace's beasts, embroidered upon the back thereof fringed with

a thin fringe of Venice gold and purple silk, having four pommels of wood gilt and two roundels of wood having in them the King's Arms or badges painted and gilt.

[14153] one bedstead carved, painted and gilt, having ceelor tester [canopy], double valances and bases of crimson damask, embroidered with borders of acorns of cloth of gold, the said ceelor and tester richly embroidered with the King's Arms within a garland crowned, held by his Majesty's beasts. The said tester fringed on both sides with a narrow fringe of Venice gold, the valances fringed with a deep fringe of Venice gold and silk lined with canvas stained red, with 5 curtains of crimson taffeta fringed on both sides and beneath with a narrow fringe of Venice gold with one bed, one bolster, two pillow and one pillow of assaye of fustian filled with down with 7 quilts of linen cloth filled with wool and two little quilts for the bed sides of linen cloth filled with wool and covered with blue velvet, one crimson damask lined with red flannel, one scarlet lined with white fustian, one fustian of white fustian and one counterpoint of crimson damask, embroidered round about with a border of cloth of gold and allouer, lozenged with cordants of Venice gold and fringed with a narrow fringer of Venice gold lined with sarsenet and four cloth sacks to truss all the said stuff in.

GAMES AND TOYS

[3227] a chessboard of ebony wrought with gold on both sides

[3228] a case of black leather containing 32 chessmen silver whereof 16 being gilt, and in the same cases 13 hens and a fox of silver gilt.

[11381] a great baby [doll], lying in a box of wood having a gown of white cloth of silver and kirtle of green velvet, the gown tied with small aglets

of gold and a small pair of beads of gold and a small chain and collar about the neck of gold

MUSICAL INSTRUMENTS

[11910] 5 flutes of ivory tipped with gold enameled black with a case of purple velvet garnished at both ends with silver and gilt

[11926] a bagpipe with pipes of ivory, the bag covered with purple velvet

[12333] a pair of virginals [keyboard instruments with strings plucked with a quill] fashioned like a harp

SUNDRY ITEMS

[1976] three forks of silver and gilt two of them having crystals in the handles [weighing] 6 oz 3 quarts

[2844] an hourglass garnished with gold

[2919] a mirror of gold having written upon it on the one side "fiat voluntas tua" ["let thy will be done"], the other side a glass

[3294] a globe or instrument of astronomy copper gilt standing upon a foot of silver gilt

[3779] boar spears with ashen staves, trimmed with crimson velvet and fringed with red silk

[9452] 7 rackets for the tennis

[14434] a two-hand sword with a scabbard of green velvet, having scallop shells upon the pommel and the cross with the said pommel partly gilt

[16021] a staff of unicorn's horns garnished with silver gilt and 9 stones in the top

[16047] a dagger garnished with silver gilt, the hilt enameled blue.

Endnotes

NOTES ON THE TEXT

Full titles and other publication details for works cited below appear in the Select Bibliography. The following abbreviations are used in these Notes:

A&M   John Foxe, *Acts and Monuments* (1838 edition)

APC   Acts of the Privy Council, Vol. II, 1547–1550

CSPS   Calendar of Letters, Despatches and State Papers relating to the Negotiations between England and Spain . . .

EM   John Strype, *Ecclesiastical Memorials* (1822)

HJ   The Historical Journal

JBS   Journal of British Studies

L&P   Letters and Papers, Foreign and Domestic, of the Reign of Henry VIII

ODNB *Oxford Dictionary of National Biography*

SoR   The Statutes of the Realm

SP   State Papers

TNA   The National Archives, Kew

FOREWORD

1   G. R. Elton, *Reform and Reformation* (1978), pp. 331–2; John Guy, *Tudor England* (1988), pp. 197–9; David Starkey, *The Reign of Henry VIII* (1995), pp. 136–142.

2   Foxe, *A&M*, Vol. VI, p. 606.

3   Elton, *Reform and Reformation*, p. 330.

4   Susan E. James (*Kateryn Parr*, p. 289), the otherwise excellent biographer of Kateryn Parr, Henry VIII's sixth wife, reiterates this point: "during the month of December, Privy Council meetings had taken place not at Westminster but at the Earl of Hertford's Somerset House." This is doubly flawed in that the Earl of Hertford was not yet the Duke of Somerset, and so his house remained called "Hertford Place," not yet "Somerset House."

5   *CSPS*, Vol. VIII, p. 534; *L&P*, Vol. XXI, Part 2, 516, 551, 595, 598, 604, 618, 629, 654: December 9 to January 2; *APC* 1542–47, pp. 559–62: from December 8 to January 2; it's unclear where they met on January 4.

6   Starkey (*Reign of Henry VIII*, pp. 137–8) asserts here that there is "incontrovertible evidence that the actual contents of the will were altered long after the date on which it was supposed to be signed . . . Sir Thomas Seymour was listed as a councillor in the will, but he was only appointed to the Privy Council on January 23."

7   Ibid.

8   Ives ("Henry VIII's Will," 1992, p. 788) spotted Starkey's mistake, but Hutchinson (*Last Days*, p. 215) repeated it. In addition, twelve members of Henry VIII's Privy Council are not listed as councillors in the will: nine of them are merely assistants, and three (Gardiner, Norfolk, and Westminster) were excluded. See Appendix II for full lists of the personnel of each council.

9   It was first alleged by Foxe (*A&M*, Vol. V, p. 689), and repeated by Elton (*Reform and Reformation*, p. 331), Lacey Baldwin Smith (*Henry VIII*, 1971, p. 271), and Hutchinson (*Last Days*, p. 217).

10 *APC*, 1547–1550, p. 18; *EM*, Vol. 2, Part I, p. 17; Herbert of Cherbury (*Life and Raigne*, 1649), p. 563.

11 *SoR*, 26 Hen. 8. c.13; Foxe, *A&M*, Vol. V, p. 689.

12 Foxe, *A&M*, Vol VI, p. 194.

13 Childs, *Henry VIII's Last Victim*.

1 THE DEATH OF A KING

1 Henry VIII had three velvet and silk-covered sedan chairs in which he could be carried around his palaces. The inventory of his possessions at his death records: "Twoo Cheyres called trauewes for the kinges Majestie to sitt in *to be carried to and fro in his galleries and Chambres* couered with tawney vellat allouer quilted with a cordaunte of taawny silke" and "an other Cheyre called a Traeuwe serving for thafforesaide purpose couered with russett vellatt allouer quilted with a cordaunte of russett silke." In addition, he had a fourth chair covered with purple velvet and silk in which he could be lifted up and down the stairs: in the words of the inventory, "one Cheyre couered with purple vellat . . . the same cheyre did serue in the kinges house that goeth upp and downe" (my italics; Starkey, Hayward, and Ward, Vol 1., p. 263, "Refuse Stuffe at Westminster in the Chardge of James Rufforth"). This latter reference is corroborated by a comment made by Elizabeth Holland, the Duke of Norfolk's mistress (now only known to us through Lord Herbert of Cherbury's history) that the king "could not go up and down the stairs, but was let up and down by a device" (Herbert of Cherbury, *Life and Reign*, 1662, p. 625).

2 De Selve, *Correspondance politique*, No. 96, pp. 88–9; CSPS, Vol. IX, p. 2; L&P, Vol. XXI, Part 2, 713, 743.

3 SoR, Vol. III, 26 Hen. VIII, c.13.

4 CSPS, Vol. IX, p. 20.

5 The account of Henry VIII's death comes from John Foxe, A&M, Vol. V, p. 689.

6 Marshall, "Death."

7   Collinson, "John Foxe as Historian."

8   Foxe, A&M, Vol. V, p. 689.

9   Lipscomb, 1536.

10 Cavendish, *Life and Death of Cardinal Wolsey*, p. 86.

11 Note that Deuteronomy (Chapter 25, Verse 6) states the polar opposite: that a man ought to marry his brother's widow.

12 Scarisbrick, Henry VIII, p. 287.

13 SoR, Vol. III, 28 Hen. VIII c.7, p. 660.

2   THE LAST DECADE

1   *L&P*, Vol. XII, Part I, 1068; ibid., Part II, 77. This has led some commentators to suggest that Henry had ulcers in both legs, but this is our only evidence to suggest it.

2   *L&P*, Vol. XII, Part I, 995.

3   Burnet, *History of the Reformation*, 1865, Vol. IV, pp. 272–85.

4   Burnet, ibid., p. 86.

5   Burnet, *History of the Reformation*, 1820, Vol. 3, Part I, p. 253; Starkey, *Rivals in Power*, p. 100.

6   *L&P*, Vol. XVI, 1334.

7   SP 1/180, f. 69; *L&P*, Vol. XVIII, Part I, 894; my spelling of her name, following her recent biographer Susan E. James, replicates how Kateryn herself spelled it.

8   BL Royal MS A X XVI, f. 45r.

9   Hutchinson, *Last Days*, p. 106.

10 *SoR*, 35 Henry. VIII, c.1, p. 955.

11 *SoR*, 34 & 35 Henry VIII, c. 1.

12 SP 1/212, f. 110v–111r; *L&P*, Vol. XX, Part II, 1030; also recorded by Hall, *Chronicle*, pp. 864–5; Marshall, "Mumpsimus and Sumpsimus," pp. 157–65.

3   THE LAST YEAR

1   See the excellent Childs, *Henry VIII's Last Victim*, for a full life of Surrey.

2   *APC*, 1542–47, p. 104.

3   Jordan, *Edward VI*, p. 49.

4   Childs, *Henry VIII's Last Victim*, pp. 239–43; Gruffydd, *Elis Gruffydd*; *L&P*, Vol. XXI, Part I, 33 (January 8, 1546).

5   Burnet, *History of the Reformation*, 1865, Vol. I, p. 534; Herbert of Cherbury, *Life and Raigne*, 1649, p. 538.

6   As his contemporary John, Lord Russell, once described his own; Willen, *John Russell*, p. 48; *L&P*, Vol. XIX, Part I, 816. See, for example, Hertford's terrible script and orthography in his letter to Paget, January 29, 1547 (SP 10/1/1).

7   *CSPS*, Vol. IX, p. 20.

8   Heralds were, and are, officers of arms, who have served the monarch since at least the thirteenth century. They originally acted as royal messengers, and they came to record and control the use of coats of arms and to organize ceremonial events.

9   SP Foreign, 1547–53, p. 490, cited by Gibbons, *Political Career*, p. 193.

10 Nott, *Works of Henry Howard*, Vol. I, p. xcvii.

11 Peter Marshall, Preface to Gibbons, *Political Career*, p. xvii.

12 David Starkey spells her name "Ann Ascue," while Diarmaid MacCulloch uses "Anne Ayscough," but neither indicates the reason for their adopted orthography. According to John Bale, who edited and published her account of her examinations, she spelt her name "Askewe," though he, curiously, does not: see Askew, *Examinations*, which contain the "Examinations" as first published by Bale in 1546 and 1547.

13 Or "God dwelleth in nothynge materyall": "The lattre examinacyon," in Askew, *Examinations*, pp. 99, 111, 106; Foxe, *A&M*, Vol. V, pp. 544–5.

14 Askew, ibid., pp. 121–2.

15 Although Thomas S. Freeman ("One Survived," p. 249) disputes that they were all "members of Parr's inner circle"; James, *Kateryn Parr*, p. 272.

16 Askewe named her torturers as Wriothesley and Rich ("The lattre examinacyon," in Askew, *Examinations*, p. 127), but Foxe's source, Knevet himself, said in the 1560s that Sir John Baker, not Rich, had been the second man.

17 Bale *et al.*, *Select Works*, p. 142; Burnet, *History of the Reformation*, 1730, Vol. I, p. 537; Foxe, *A&M*, Vol. V, p. 547; "The lattre examinacyon," in Askew, *Examinations*, p. 127.

18 Starkey, *Reign of Henry VIII*, p. 119; Freeman, "One Survived," p. 250; Foxe, *A&M*, Vol. V, p. 548. Also see J. G. Nichols, *Narratives of the Days of the Reformation*, p. 306. According to Foxe, Knevet was so concerned about the illegality of the action that he rushed to tell Henry what had transpired, though this may have been more out of fear of the consequences of having disobeyed Wriothesley than anything else.

19 "The lattre examinacyon," in Askew, *Examinations*, p. 130.

20 *L&P*, Vol. XXI, Part II, 1383 [72]; Ryrie, *The Gospel and Henry VIII*, p. 56.

21 *L&P*, ibid. [49]; Wabuda, "Shaxton."

22 Blage himself made this play on words to Henry, saying: "if your majesty had not been better to me than your bishops were, your pig had been roasted ere this time" (according to Foxe, *A&M*, Vol. V, p. 564).

23 Thomas S. Freeman has recently (in "One Survived") made a plausible case, based on the work of David Starkey, for putting Kateryn Parr's brush with Wriothesley before the attack on Askewe. The evidence he adduces seems to me, however, to create a case for Parr being under suspicion either in April or in July, and does not decisively indicate in which of those two months the incident occurred. While Foxe's ordering of events is not entirely reliable, given that it is the only evidence for the Parr case, it seems, on balance, most sensible to stick with his situating of the affair after the Askewe and Blage arrests. It also makes sense that Wriothesley's campaign was attempted over a short period of weeks, from Askewe's prosecution

for heresy on June 28 to some point in late-mid July. By July 25, Henry was ordering "almaner juelles, perlles, precious stones, as well set in gold . . . ffurres of sables . . . clothes . . . for the pleasure of us [and] our dearest wief, the Quene" (*L&P*, Vol. XXI, Part I, 1383 [96]).

24 Foxe, *A&M*, Vol. V, pp. 553–61.

25 Ibid., p. 556.

26 We are told, however (by Foxe, ibid., p. 558), that he only did so when sent to the queen because she was sick with melancholy, fear and agony, induced in her by the revelations of the articles; so perhaps there is some truth to the story of the serendipitously misplaced document. Certainly, Kateryn must have been in a notably bad way for Henry to send one of his own physicians. Kateryn was more usually attended by Dr. Robert Huicke (Hamilton, *The Household of Queen Katherine Parr*, pp. 57–8).

27 It has even been speculated that the parallels between the two speeches suggest that Shakespeare might have read and used Foxe as his inspiration (James, *Kateryn Parr*, p. 278, n. 84). Cf. Shakespeare, *The Taming of the Shrew*, Act V, Scene II, lines 142–85, especially lines 152–3 ("Thy husband is thy lord, thy life, thy keeper,/Thy head, thy sovereign") with Foxe, *A&M*, Vol. V, p. 559.

28 Foxe, ibid.

29 Starkey (*Reign of Henry VIII*, p. 130) states that Wriothesley's attempt to arrest the queen took place in the gardens of Hampton Court, assuming it took place in July or August. All the information we have on location from Foxe—our only source—is that they were at Whitehall. In *Six Wives* (pp. 761–4), Starkey changed his mind and placed the incident in March 1546.

30 Foxe, Vol. V, p. 561.

31 Scepticism about the story has been expressed by Ryrie (*The Gospel and Henry VIII*, p. 56), Bernard (*King's Reformation*, p. 592) and especially Redworth (*In Defence of the Catholic Church*, pp. 233–4).

32 Foxe, *A&M*, Vol. V, p. 558; see Freeman ("One Survived," pp. 238–43) for a discussion of historians' grounds for acceptance or rejection of Foxe's account, and for his own conclusions in its favor; Gibbons, *Political Career*, pp. 186–9.

33 Freeman, "One Survived," pp. 243–5; Burnet (*History of the Reformation*, 1865, Vol. I, p. 541) repeats Foxe's claim.

34 Burnet, ibid.

4   THE FINAL MONTHS

1   Hall, *Chronicle*, p. 867.

2   Hertford rejoined the meetings of Privy Council on August 1, 1546, Lisle on August 15 (*APC*, 1547–1550, pp. 501, 514).

3   *CSPS*, Vol. VIII, pp. 533–4.

4   Guy, *Tudor England*, pp. 196–9; Starkey, *Reign of Henry VIII*, pp. 132–43; Hutchinson, *Last Days*, pp. 209–16.

5   *CSPS*, Vol. VIII, p. 534.

6   Burnet (*History of the Reformation*, 1865, Vol. I, p. 542) notes that the Parr incident alienated the king so that he could never again endure the sight of Gardiner. Elton (*Reform and Reformation*, p. 330) and Susan Brigden (*New Worlds*, p. 138) are among those who have adopted this line. Redworth (*In Defence of the Catholic Church*, pp. 237–40) and Childs (*Henry VIII's Last Victim*, p. 260) are among those who note Wriothesley's pivotal role and Gardiner's ongoing royal favor until November 1546.

7   Redworth, *In Defence of the Catholic Church*, pp. 237–9.

8   De Selve to d'Annebaut, November 4, 1546 (De Selve, *Correspondance politique*, p. 51).

9   *CSPS*, Vol. VIII, p. 556.

10 As Foxe called him (e.g., *A&M*, Vol. V, p. 261).

11 Foxe, *A&M*, Vol. VI, pp. 163–4.

12 This is according to testimony in the same trial (1551) by John Dudley, who was by this time Earl of Warwick (Foxe, *A&M*, Vol. VI, p. 179). Colin Armstrong, in his article "English Catholicism

Rethought," suggests that Gardiner had crypto-papist sympathies.

13 Gardiner to Somerset, June 6, 1547 (Gardiner, *Letters*, pp. 286–7; also Foxe, *A&M*, Vol. VI, p. 36).

14 Gibbons, *Political Career*, p. 195.

15 Heal, *Of Prelates and Princes*, pp. 114–5, 123; cf., for example, SP 4/1/19 item 85, payment to the Archbishop of Canterbury for exchange of lands, November 1545.

16 Gardiner to Henry VIII, December 2, 1546 (Gardiner, *Letters*, pp. 246–8).

17 Foxe, *A&M*, Vol. VI, pp. 138–9.

18 Gibbons (*Political Career*, p. 196) suggests that as a result Gardiner was out of politics for the next month or so, as well as removed from the will, but the meaning of this is unclear: Gardiner was often not at the Privy Council—for example, the last time he attended before this incident was on October 5, 1546 (*APC*, 1542–47, p. 534).

19 Starkey, *Reign of Henry VIII*, p. 132; Ives, "Henry" VIII's Will," 1992, p. 796; Elton, *Reform and Reformation*, p. 330; also Scarisbrick, *Henry VIII*, p. 490.

20 *APC*, 1547–50, p. 16 (February 6, 1547).

21 *L&P*, Vol. XX, Part II, 610. The full line is: "Ye told mc oones ye love no extremites and the meane is best, as the wife confessed to her husband who could hitte it," which reads like a sixteenth-century joke whose meaning is lost.

22 *L&P*, Vol. VII, 20; Gammon, *Statesman and Schemer*, p. 26.

23 *State Papers of Henry VIII*, Vol. X, p. 745; *L&P*, Vol. XX, Part II, 917; Gibbons, *Political Career*, p. 163 n. 34.

24 As Samuel Rhea Gammon does, *Statesman and Schemer*, p. 115.

25 North would go on to be part of the commission for the suppression of Protestant heresy under Mary I. Starkey implies that we can tell Paget operated without Henry's knowledge because the document is stamped not signed (*Reign of Henry VIII*, p. 133); but after September

1545, *every* document requiring Henry's authorization was stamped rather than signed, so this is irrelevant.

26 *CSPS*, Vol. IX, p. 20.

27 Foxe, *A&M*, Vol. V, p. 691.

28 Burnet, *History of the Reformation* (1820 ed), Vol. III, p. 253.

29 *L&P*, Vol. V, 1059.

30 Susan Brigden ("Henry Howard") and David Starkey (*Reign of Henry VIII*, p. 135) argue this. Herbert of Cherbury, too, thought Surrey and Norfolk had been "exposed to the malignity and detraction of their accusers" (*Life and Reign*, 1662, p. 624).

31 Herbert of Cherbury (ibid.), p. 629; Brigden (ibid.), p. 534.

32 *CSPS*, Vol. VIII, pp. 534, 556.

33 SP 1/227, f. 129.

34 *CSPS*, Vol. VIII, p. 534.

35 See Elton, *Reform and Reformation*, p. 330; James, *Kateryn Parr*, p. 289.

36 *CSPS*, Vol. VIII, p. 534; *L&P*, Vol. XXI, Part II, 516, 551, 595, 598, 604, 618, 629, 654 (December 9 to January 2); *APC*, 1542–47, pp. 559–62 (December 8 to January 2). It is unclear where they met on January 4.

37 *L&P*, Vol. XXI, Part 2, 546; Childs (*Henry VIII's Last Victim*, p. 270) says that Surrey spent the first ten days of this confinement at Wriothesley's house, from December 2, 1546; Ives, "Henry VIII's Will," 1994, p. 908.

38 The idea that Wriothesley jumped ship in late 1546 to ally with the reformers—as posited by Gibbons (*Political Career*, p. 190) and implied by Ives ("Henry VIII's Will," 1992: that he "began trim to the way the wind was blowing," p. 783)—has no evidential base beyond the inscrutable memo.

39 Diarmaid MacCulloch (*Thomas Cranmer*, p. 339) agrees: "they hardly needed a Machivellian conspiracy to establish their supremacy when their enemies handed it to them on a plate."

40 Herbert of Cherbury, *Life and Reign*, 1662, p. 625; *L&P*, Vol. XXI, Part 2, 555, 697.

41 Jessie Childs (*Henry VIII's Last Victim*, p. 286) argues that
    Surrey did, in fact, have a valid claim to bear the arms of
    Edward the Confessor. Still, Elton's judgment that there is
    "slender proof" for Surrey's guilt is mistaken: at least two of
    these provocations were (or could be construed to be) treasonous
    under the Treasons Act of 1534 and the Succession Act of 1536;
    they were all affronts.

42 Freeman, "One Survived," p. 251.

43 SP 1/227, f. 123; my italics.

44 *L&P*, Vol. XII, Part 2, 541; Bindoff (*History of Parliament*, Vol. III,
    p. 353) opines that Southwell probably ratted on Surrey in order to
    "ingratiate himself with the King and the rising house of
    Seymour."

45 Brigden, "Henry Howard," pp. 514–15; Childs, *Henry VIII's Last
    Victim*, pp. 258–9, 292–3. Both Surrey and Askewe were para-
    phrasing the first five chapters of Ecclesiastes, but compare the treat-
    ment of lines 44–6 of Chapter 3. In Surrey they read:

I saw a royal throne whereas that Justice should have sit;
Instead of whom, I saw, with fierce and cruel mode,
Where Wrong was set, that bloody beast, that drunk the guiltless blood.

Askewe rendered them:

I saw a royal throne,
Where justice should have sit,
But in her stead was one
Of moody, cruel wit.
Absorbed was righteousness,
As of the raging flood:
Satan, in his excess,
Sucked up the guiltless blood.

It is impossible to believe (as per Starkey, *Reign of Henry VIII*, p. 126) that by this point Surrey had probably "become as conservative as his father."

46 Herbert of Cherbury, *Life and Reign*, 1662, pp. 629–30; Gammon, *Statesman and Schemer*, p. 73.
47 *CSPS*, Vol. IX, p. 3; *L&P*, Vol. XXI, Part 2, 697; Herbert of Cherbury, ibid., p. 626.
48 *L&P*, Vol. XXI, Part 2, 753.
49 Burnet, *History of the Reformation*, 1865, Vol. I, p. 544.

5   THE MAKING OF THE WILL

1 *CSPS*, Vol. VIII, p. 320, although I think Baldwin Smith ("The Last Will," p. 14) is overstating it to say that "three times" in 1546 (March, October, and December) "Henry had approached death and drawn away." Henry was ill, but he does not seem to have been on the point of death before January 1547.
2 Although we are most familiar with colic as something that babies suffer from, it is, in fact, an intense pain in humans of any age, or animals too, caused by muscular contractions in response to an obstruction in the digestive tract, gall bladder, or other internal tube. *L&P*, Vol. XXI, Part 1, 1227; De Selve to Francis I, July 8, 1546 (De Selve, *Correspondance politique*, p. 7).
3 De Selve to Francis I, September 8 and October 28, 1546 (ibid., pp. 25, 47).
4 De Selve to Francis I, November 25, 1546 (ibid, pp. 60–1); *L&P*, Vol. XXI, Part 2, 517.
5 *CSPS*, Vol. VIII, p. 533; *L&P*, Vol. XXI, Part 2, 605, 606.
6 *APC*, 1547–1550, p. 18; Foxe, *A&M*, Vol. VI, pp. 163, 177. Paget remembers all seven of them being in attendance; Lisle remembered only himself, Hertford, Paget, Russell, and Browne.

7 Jessie Childs has carefully observed that it is possible that "secretary" simply meant that Wriothesley had been the scribe, rather than refer to his actual post as secretary; but that would make the sentence tautologous ("written with the hand of the lord Wriothsley, being secretary") and therefore seems unlikely.

8 John Guy (*Tudor England*, pp. 198–9, 481), following Dale Hoak, argues that there were two wills, which are, he implies, substantively different: one housed at the Inner Temple, dated December 13, 1546 (Petyt MS 538/47, ff. 398–406), and the one at the National Archives, dated December 30, 1546 (TNA E/23/4). Eric Ives ("Henry VIII's Will," 1992, pp. 780–1) proved that the Inner Temple one is not an earlier, different will, but instead a copy of the will of December 30, and that the scribe misheard the date. Ives also demonstrates that a comparison of the two documents indicates no differences of substance between them.

9 Foxe, *A&M*, Vol. VI, p. 163.

10 Ibid.; BL Harley MS 849, f. 32r.

11 Sturge, *Cuthbert Tunstal*, pp. 1–25.

12 *L&P*, Vol. X, 797.

13 Willen, *John Russell*, pp. 4–40.

14 Henry VII had included both the chief justices of the King's Bench and the Common Pleas in his list of executors (Astle, *Will of King Henry*, p. 42). Perhaps the presence of Sir Edward Montagu on the Council, who had been Lord Chief Justice of the King's Bench until 1545, was felt to be sufficient. Sir Thomas Bromley would rise to become the Lord Chief Justice of the King's Bench himself in October 1553.

15 John Spelman, *Reports,* edited by J. H. Baker (Selden Society, 94, 1978), Vol. II, p. 360, cited by Ives, "Henry VIII's Will," 1992, p. 801.

16 Foxe, *A&M*, Vol. VI, p. 163.

17 *CSPS*, 1547–9, pp. 340–1; Foxe, *A&M*, Vol. VI, p. 164; Ives, "Henry VIII's Will," 1992, p. 789.

18 Foxe, *A&M*, Vol. VI, pp. 163, 170; Vol. V, pp. 691–2; Burnet, *History of the Reformation*, 1865, Vol. I, p. 548.

19 SP 4/1/19, item 85; BL Harley MS 849, f. 32r.

20 Baldwin Smith, *Henry VIII*, p. 11, but he does not provide any evidence to support this assertion; *L&P*, Vol. XXI, Part 2, 648 item 16.

21 SP 4/1/19 item 85.

22 See discussion of the dry stamp by Ives ("Henry VIII's Will," 1992, pp. 782–8); Starkey ("Court and Government," p. 55).

23 *L&P*, Vol. XXI, Part 1 (1536), 31, 32, 33; (1537), 34.

24 SP 4/1.

25 SP 4/1/19, item 85; BL Harley MS 849, f. 32v. The claim by W. K. Jordan—that he, A. J. Pollard and Lacey Baldwin Smith, having examined the original will, were unpersuaded that Henry had not personally signed it—is barely plausible (Jordan, *Edward VI*, p. 55; Pollard, *England Under Protector Somerset*, p. 5, though Baldwin Smith, "The Last Will," pp. 22–3, is more circumspect). Had Henry signed it himself, there would have been no need subsequently to include the will in the register of documents signed by dry stamp, nor would its stamping have been sworn to later by Paget. Cf. Ives, "Henry VIII's Will," 1992, p. 782.

26 BL Harley MS 849; Letter from Sir William Maitland, Lord of Ledington (Lethington), Secretary of Scotland to Sir William Cecil, January 4, 1566, in Egerton, *Egerton Papers*, pp. 41–9.

27 Egerton, ibid., pp. 46–7. Both David Starkey (*Reign of Henry VIII*, pp. 133–8) and John Guy (*Tudor England*, pp. 198–9) are of this view.

28 Starkey, ibid., p. 140.

29 Ibid.

30 Ives ("Henry VIII's Will," 1994, p. 904) also makes this argument.

31 Starkey, *Reign of Henry VIII*, p. 138.

32 *L&P*, Vol. XXI, Part 2, 331.

33 De Selve and La Garde to Francis I, January 10, 1547 (De Selve, *Correspondance politique*, p. 81); *L&P*, Vol. XXI, Part 2, 684.

34   Foxe, *A&M*, Vol. VI, p. 189; De Selve and La Garde to Francis I, January 15, 1547 (De Selve, *Correspondance politique*, pp. 86–7).

6   THE FAITH OF THE KING

1   Lloyd, *Formularies of Faith*, p. 215.

2   MacCulloch (*Thomas Cranmer*, pp. 356–8) and Scarisbrick (*Henry VIII*, pp. 469–70) are two of the few historians who mention this. Bertano's appearance is secretive in the sources: *L&P*, Vol. XXI, Part 1, 1339; De Selve, *Correspondance politique*, p. 17.

3   Foxe, *A&M*, Vol. V, pp. 563–4; Starkey, *Reign of Henry VIII*, p. 130; Scarisbrick, *Henry VIII*, p. 472; MacCulloch, *Thomas Cranmer*, p. 357.

4   Foxe, *A&M*, Vol. V, p. 564; Gibbons, *Political Career*, p. 167.

5   Ives, "Henry VIII's Will," 1992, p. 797; Bindoff, *Tudor England*, pp. 149–50; Lockyer, *Tudor and Stuart Britain*, p. 105.

6   Elton, *Henry VIII*, pp. 25–6; Baldwin Smith ("Henry VIII and the Protestant Triumph," p. 1243) considered this at some length.

7   Beem, "Have not wee a noble kynge?," p. 220; Bernard, *King's Reformation*, p. 591.

8   Muller, *Stephen Gardiner*, p. 87, citing Gardiner, *A declaration of such true articles as George Joye hath gone about to confute as false* (London, 1546), ff. 8–11.

9   Bernard (*King's Reformation*, p. 594), strangely, says that there are "no bequests or requests to the Virgin Mary," which is patently wrong.

10   Astle, *Will of King Henry*, p. 3; Wooding, *Henry VIII*, p. 272. Henry VII mentions "Saint Michaell, Saint John Baptist, Saint Johon Evuangelist, Saint George, Saint Anthony, Saint Edward, Saint Vincent, Saint Anne, Saint Marie Magdalene, and Saint Barbara" and says "thi moost Blissed Moder evir Virgyne, oure Lady Saincte Mary; in whom after the in this mortall lif, hath ever been my moost singulier trust and confidence, to whom in al my necessities I

have made my continuel refuge, and by whom I have hiderto in all myn advertisities, ever had my sp'ial comforte and relief" etc.

11 TNA PROB 11/40/40, January 28, 1558, Will of Steven [*sic*] Gardiner, Bishop of Winchester.

12 TNA PROB 11/32/514, September 19, 1549, Will of Sir Anthony Denny; PROB 11/32/121, May 11, 1548, Will of Sir William Parr; PROB 11/34/154, May 14, 1551, Will of Thomas, Earl Southampton of [*sic*].

13 TNA PROB 11/32/514; PROB 11/34/154; PROB 11/40/40.

14 According to medieval Catholics, purgatory was a place of purging to which the soul went after death, where the sinner had an opportunity to pay off the remaining debt for his or her sin. The soul's journey through purgatory could be hastened in life by the performance of penances or the receiving of "indulgences"—certificates issued by the pope, granting time off purgatory in reward for good works—or, after death, by the prayers of others. The Reformation began with Martin Luther's protest against indulgences in 1517, and Protestants soon abandoned the notion of purgatory, decrying it as unscriptural. The amount Henry VIII left for prayers for his soul is still less, however, than his father's legacy of £2,000 to be given in alms for "the weale of our soule . . . to th'entent thei [the receipients of alms] doo prai to Almighty God for the remission of our synnes, and salvacion of our Soule" (Astle, *Will of King Henry*, p. 9).

7 THE SUCCESSION

1 *SoR*, Vol. III, 28 Hen. VIII c.7, pp. 656–62; 35 Hen VIII c.1, pp. 955–8.

2 *SoR* III, 35 Hen VIII c.1, p. 955.

3 Henry VIII's only provision for the future was for the marriage of his daughter Mary to the Prince of Spain. His will provided her with a dowry of £50,000, which was to be supplied to her even should the marriage fail to be effected (Astle, *Will of King Henry*,

pp. 38–41); he makes no mention of his direct heir. Cf. also J. Nichols, *A Collection*: Henry V's will (pp. 236–42) and Henry VI's will (pp. 291–319).

4   Ives, *Lady Jane Grey*, pp. 39–40.

5   J. Nichols, *A Collection*: Henry V's will (pp. 236–42) and Henry VI's will (pp. 291–319); Astle, *Will of King Henry*.

6   Guy, *My Heart is My Own*, p. 53. It may also be that Henry was disbarring Marie de Guise's heir out of spite because Marie de Guise had chosen to marry Henry's nephew, James V of Scotland, rather than Henry himself, in the marital interval between Jane Seymour and Anne of Cleves.

7   Griffiths, "Minority of Henry VI," pp. 161, 163.

8   *SoR*, Vol. III, 28 Hen. VIII c.7, p. 661.

9   Baldwin Smith, "Last Will and Testament," p. 17.

10 Ibid., pp. 19, 20, 25.

11 Foxe, *A&M*, Vol. VI, p. 189.

12 Dodd, "Richard II," p. 108.

13 Ibid., p. 131.

14 Machiavelli's text was completed by 1513, and may well have circulated in manuscript before its actual publication.

15 I am grateful to Dr. Joanne Paul for sharing her thoughts on this with me: cf. her Ph.D thesis "Counsel and Command in English Political Thought, 1485–1651" (Queen Mary, University of London, 2013).

8   THE TRANSFER OF POWER

1   *EM*, Vol. 2, Part I, p. 18.

2   Burnet, *History of the Reformation*, 1865, Vol. I, p. 550; *CSPS*, Vol. IX, p. 6.

3   Ives, "Henry VIII's Will," 1994, p. 908.

4   BL Cotton Titus F III, in *EM*, Vol. 2, Part II, Appendix HH, p. 430 (109).

5   *EM*, Vol. 2, Part I, p. 17.

6 *CSPS*, Vol. VIII, p. 557.

7 BL Cotton Titus F III, in *EM*, Vol. 2, Part II, Appendix GG, p. 427, and Appendix HH, p. 433 (III).

8 Edward VI, *Chronicle and Political Papers*, p. 4.

9 Ibid.; Sir John Hayward, *Life and Raigne of King Edward the Sixth* (first published in 1630, though circulating in manuscript before that), p. 34.

10 Letter from Edward Seymour, Earl of Hertford to Sir William Paget (Tytler, *England under the Reigns*, Vol. I, pp. 15–16).

11 Sir John Hayward, *Life and Reign*, p. 36. The general pardon was indeed issued at Edward's coronation, although half a dozen names were excluded from its benevolence.

12 Letter from Hertford to Paget and the Council, January 29, 1547 (TNA SP 10/1/1).

13 On February 7, 1547, Edward VI wrote to the dowager queen from the Tower expressing their common grief at the death of "my father and your husband, the most illustrious King" and wishing her "great good health" (Parr, *Complete Works*, pp. 128–9).

14 Letter from William Wightman, former servant of Sir Anthony Browne to Mr. Cecill, 10 May 1549 (Tytler, *England under the Reigns*, Vol. I, p. 169).

15 BL Add. MS 71009, f. 45r.

16 J. G. Nichols, *Literary Remains of King Edward*, Vol. I, pp. 86–7.

17 *APC*, Vol. II, pp. 3–4.

18 Ibid., p. 7.

19 Ibid., p. 5.

20 Jordan (*Edward VI*, pp. 57–8) and Hoak (*King's Council*, p. 231) believed it overthrew the will; Elton (*Reform and Reformation*, p. 333), Loades (*John Dudley*, p. 87) and Ives ("Henry VIII's Will," 1992, p. 803) believed it conformed entirely to Henry's provisions, and that it was foreseeable.

21 *APC*, Vol. II, p. 5.

9 THE "UNWRITTEN WILL"

1 TNA PROB 11/40/40; PROB 11/32/19.

2 Rymer (*Foedera*) has "cabels" for "cabettes," and certainly cables would be an easy word to understand in the context of ships, but the correct transcription is definitely "cabettes." It seems likely to be "sabot" (from the Old French *çabot*; see the *Oxford English Dictionary*), meaning the block at the base of a cannon or device fitted into the muzzle of a gun to support it while loading. This would fit with it appearing after "artillery, ordnance, munitions, ships . . ." although is still frightfully specific. I am grateful to Paul Barnes, Allan Draycott, and Caroline Shenton for their input on this.

3 Starkey, Hawkyard and Ward, *Inventory of King Henry*, p. xi.

4 Ibid., p. x.

5 Astle, *Will of King Henry*, pp. 38–41.

6 Hutchinson (*Last Days*, p. 214) states that 500 marks equaled £650, implying that Cranmer was given more than anyone else. In fact, a mark was worth two-thirds of a pound, or 13s. 4d., so 500 marks was *less* than £500: £333 4s.

7 Except possibly Edward Bellingham, who became a Gentleman of the Privy Chamber to Edward VI.

8 *APC*, Vol. II, 1547–50 (p. 147) for example warrants the payment on November 28, 1547 of £200 to Sir Richard Rich, "for so miche bequethed to him by the Kinges Majeste deceased."

9 I am grateful to Dr. Lars Kjaer for this point. Cf. the will of Henry V, who instructs his executors to make "paiement of my dettes"; that of Henry VI, who asks his "to do plain and entire execution of my last will and testament, in the which I will that the debts of my household be specially preferred"; and that of Henry VII: "we wol, that all our debts furst and before al other charges . . . with all possible spede and diligence after thei appere due, justely and truly bee contented and paied, by the hands of oure Executours, wherewith we charge theim as thei wol aunswere for us before God, and discharge our conscience.

And also if any p'sone of what degree soevir he bee, shewe by way of complainte to our Executours, any wrong to have been doon to hym, by us, our commaundement, occasion or meane, or that we helde any goodes or lands which of right ought to apperteigne unto hym; we wol that every such complainte, be spedely, tenderly and effectuelly herde . . . as the caas shall require, he and thei bee restored and recompensed by our said Executours, of such our redy money and juelx as then shall remayne" and "we wol if any p'sone prove before our Executours, that any dutie is owing unto hym . . . then our said Executours take suche provision for his contentacion, that he be paied." Quotations from J. Nichols, *A Collection*: Henry V, p. 236, and Henry VI, p. 309; Astle, *Will of King Henry*, pp. 11–13. Cf. Houlbrooke ("Debate," p. 895), who argues that it was an "extremely unusual clause."

10 Burnet, *History of the Reformation*, 1865, Vol. I, p. 550; Herbert of Cherbury, *Life and Reign*, p. 631; *L&P*, Vol. XXI, Part 2, 647 (item 25); 648 (items 43 and 51); 771 (item 14).

11 *L&P*, ibid., 648 (item 50).

12 *APC*, Vol. II, 1547–50, p. 16.

13 Ibid., p. 17.

14 Ibid., p. 19.

15 Ibid.

16 *Calendar of the Patent Rolls: Edward VI, I, 1547–48*, p. 173.

17 Houlbrooke, "Debate," pp. 895–9; Starkey, *Reign of Henry VIII*, pp. 141–2; Elton, *Reform and Reformation*, p. 333.

18 TNA SP 10/1/28.

19 Ives, "Henry VIII's Will," 1994, p. 905.

20 Ibid., p. 906.

21 Elton, *Reform and Reformation*, p. 333; *CSPS*, Vol. IX, p. 4.

22 Ives, "Henry VIII's Will," 1994, p. 906.

23 Miller, "Henry VIII's Unwritten Will," p. 88.

24 TNA SP 10/1/41.

25 *Calendar of the Patent Rolls: Edward VI, I, 1547–48*, pp. 7, 17, 18,
    21–4, 25–33, 173, 240, etc. Miller notes ("Henry VIII's Unwritten
    Will," p. 96), however, that neither Sir John St. Leger nor Sir Chris-
    topher Danby were actually ennobled.

26 *APC*, Vol. II, 1547–50, p. 41.

10 THE LEGACY OF THE WILL

1   Edward VI, *Chronicle and Political Papers*, p. 4; cf. Sir John Hay-
    ward, *Life and Raigne*, p. 35.

2   Van der Delft to the Queen Dowager, February 10, 1547
    (*CSPS*, Vol. IX, p. 19).

3   BL Add. MS 48126, f. 15a–b; Gibbons, *Political Career*,
    p. 217.

4   Skidmore, *Edward VI*, p. 64; Ives, "Henry VIII's Will," 1992,
    p. 803.

5   *APC*, Vol. II, 1547–50, p. 48.

6   Ibid., p. 55.

7   Ibid., p. 56.

8   Ibid.

9   Ibid., pp. 63–4; Beem, "Have not wee a noble kynge?," p. 224; Elton,
    Reform and Reformation, p. 334.

10 *APC*, Vol. II, 1547–50, p. 68.

11 *EM*, Vol. 2, Part II, p. 112.

12 E/23/4, ff. 23, 20.

13 MacCulloch, *Tudor Church Militant*, pp. 50–1.

14 Stow, *Annales*, p. 601; Hoak, *King's Council*, pp. 55, 96; Ives, "Henry
    VIII's Will," 1992, p. 792.

15 Inner Temple Library, Petyt MS 538/47, f. 317.

16 Ives, *Lady Jane Grey*, pp. 137–49.

17 *CSPS*, Vol. IX, p. 70; Houlbrooke, "Debate," p. 897; letter from
    Mary I to her councillors, July 9, 1553, signed "Marye the quene"
    (Inner Temple, Petyt MS 538/47).

18 Whitelock, *Mary Tudor*, p. 301.

19 Letter from Sir William Maitland, Lord of Ledington (Lethington), Secretary of Scotland to Sir William Cecil, January 4, 1566 (Egerton, *Egerton Papers*, pp. 41–9).

20 BL Harley MS 849, f. 31v; BL Harley MS 419, ff. 150v–151r, dated 20 March 1565; Miller, "Henry VIII's Unwritten Will," p. 94.

21 BL Harley MS 849, ff. 32r, 37r.

22 *APC*, Vol. II, 1547–50, p. 59; BL Harley MS 849, ff. 32rv.

23 SP 12/7, f. 71; Baldwin Smith, "Last Will and Testament," p. 25.

24 SP 11/4, f. 93; Baldwin Smith, ibid.

EPILOGUE

1 Starkey, *Reign of Henry VIII*, p. 143.

2 Redworth, *In Defence of the Catholic Church*, p. 243, n. 46.

3 *APC*, Vol. II, 1547–50, p. 41.

APPENDIX I

1 For example, "bodyes" is regularly corrected to "bodies," "Edwarde" to "Edward," "sayde" to "said," "sonne" to "son," etc.—although sometimes when it does say "said," Rymer has curiously changed it to "sayd," "stuff" to "stuffe" or "until" to "untill," and so forth.

2 Rymer has "commandeth."

3 Rymer omits "the."

4 Meaning "realm," cf. *OED* early pronunciation and spelling.

5 Rymer has "folk."

6 This repeat is in the original.

7 An interstitial insertion.

8 Rymer says "several."

9 Rymer has "our defoult."

10 Rymer has "and for our."

11 Rymer has "Catheryn."

12 Rymer omits "said."

13 An interstitial insertion.

14 Another interstitial insertion, this time struck through.

15 Rymer says "the condition."

16 Rymer says "or."

17 Rymer omits these five words.

18 Rymer has (as Ives observes) "do not kepe."

19 Rymer has "Lady Eliz."

20 Rymer omits the "c" from "Peckham."

21 Rymer has "cabels."

22 "Realme" is missing from Rymer.

23 Rymer has "archebushop."

24 Rymer has "because."

25 Rymer has "graunt them."

26 Rymer has "and" instead of "or."

27 Throughout, 500 is written "V" with a superscript mark like a cross.

28 A large space is left after each recipient.

29 Rymer says 540.

30 Rymer adds: "Tom. VI. P. III."

31 Rymer has "Mentes," but this is Sir Peter Mewtas.

32 The will is damaged here, and for seven lines below, so the sums in square brackets are gleaned from another copy.

Bibliography

PRIMARY SOURCES (IN MANUSCRIPT)

British Library: Add. MS 48126; Add. MS 71009; Harley MS
419; Harley MS 849; Royal MS A X XVI.

Inner Temple: Petyt MS 538/47.

The National Archives: E/23/4; SP 1/212; SP 4/1/19, Documents
stamped under Henry VIII's dry stamp, 1545–7; SP 10/1; SP 10/1/1,
Letter from Hertford to Paget and the Council, January 29, 1547;
SP 10/1/17; SP 10/1/28; SP 10/1/41; SP 10/3/7; SP 10/8/4; PROB
11/32/19, Will of Katherine Parr; PROB 11/32/121, May 11, 1548, Will
of Sir William Parr; PROB 11/32/514, September 19, 1549, Will of
Sir Anthony Denny; PROB 11/34/154, May 14, 1551, Will of
Thomas, Earl Southampton of; PROB 11/40/40, January 28, 1558,
Will of Steven Gardiner, Bishop of Winchester.

PRIMARY SOURCES (PRINTED)

Acts of the Privy Council, ed. J. R. Dasent (London, 1890–1907), Vol. II, *1547–
1550* [APC]

ASKEW, ANNE, *The Examinations of Anne Askew*, edited by Elaine V.
Beilin (Oxford and New York, 1996)

ASTLE, T. (ed.), *The Will of King Henry VII* (London, 1775)

BALE, JOHN *et al.*, *Select Works of John Bale Containing the Examinations of Lord Cobham, William Thorpe, and Anne Askewe and the Images of Both Churches*, edited by Henry Christmas (Cambridge, 1849)

BURNET, GILBERT, *The History of the Reformation of the Church of England*, 3 vols (Dublin, 1730)

————, *The History of the Reformation of the Church of England*, 6 vols (London, 1820)

————, *The History of the Reformation of the Church of England*, edited by Nicholas Pocock, 7 vols (Oxford, 1865)

Calendar of the Patent Rolls: Edward VI, Vol I, *1547–48* (London, 1924)

Calendar of Letters, Despatches and State Papers relating to the Negotiations Between England and Spain, Vol. VIII (*Henry VIII, 1545–1546*), edited by M.A.S Hume, and Vol. IX (*Edward VI, 1547–1549*), edited by M.A.S. Hume and R. Tytler (London 1904 and 1912) [*CLSP*]

CAVENDISH, GEORGE, "The Life and Death of Cardinal Wolsey," in *Two Early Tudor Lives*, edited by Richard S. Sylvester and Davis P. Harding (New Haven, Conn., and London, 1962)

DE SELVE, ODET, *Correspondance politique de Odet de Selve, ambassadeur de France en Angleterre*, edited by G. Lefèvre-Pontalis (Paris, 1888)

EDWARD VI, *The Chronicle and Political Papers of King Edward VI*, edited by W. K. Jordan (London, 1966)

EGERTON, SIR THOMAS, *The Egerton Papers: A Collection of Public and Private Documents, chiefly illustrative of the times of Elizabeth and James I, from the original manuscripts, the property of the Right Hon. Lord Francis Egerton*, edited by J. Payne Collier (London, 1840)

FOXE, JOHN, *Acts and Monuments*, edited by S. R. Cattley (London, 1838)

GARDINER, STEPHEN, *The Letters of Stephen Gardiner*, edited by J. A. Muller (Cambridge, 1933)

Gruffydd, Elis, *Elis Gruffydd and the 1544 "Enterprises" of Paris and Boulogne*, edited by Jonathan Davies, translated by M. B. Davies (Farnham, Surrey, 2003)

HALL, EDWARD, *Hall's Chronicle, Containing the History of England* . . .
    (London, 1809)

HAYWARD, SIR JOHN, *The Life and Raigne of King Edward the Sixth*,
    edited by Barrett L. Beer (Kent, Ohio, 1993)

HERBERT OF CHERBURY, *The Life and Raigne of King Henry the Eighth*
    (London, 1649)

———, *The Life and Reign of King Henry the Eighth* (London, 1662)

HUGHES, JOHN AND WHITE KENNETT, *A Complete History of England with
    the Lives of All the Kings and Queens Thereof*, 3 vols (London, 1706)

Letters and Papers, Foreign and Domestic, of the Reign of Henry VIII,
    edited by J. S Brewer, James Gairdner and R. H. Brodie, 21 vols
    (London, 1862–1932) [*L&P*]

LLOYD, C., *Formularies of Faith* (Oxford, 1856)

NICHOLS, JOHN, *A Collection of All The Wills Now Known to be Extant
    of the Kings and Queens of England, Princes and Princess of Wales,
    and Every Branch of the Blood Royal, From the Reign of William the
    Conqueror to That of Henry the Seventh Exclusive* (London, 1780)

NICHOLS, JOHN GOUGH (ed.), *Literary Remains of King Edward the
    Sixth*, 2 vols (London, 1857)

———, (ed.), *Narratives of the Days of the Reformation* (London, 1859)

NOTT, G. F. (ed.), *Works of Henry Howard, Earl of Surrey and of Sir
    Thomas Wyatt the Elder*, 2 vols (London, 1815–16)

PARR, KATHERINE, *Complete Works and Correspondence*, edited by Janel
    Mueller, (Chicago and London, 2011)

RYMER, THOMAS, *Foedera*, 3rd edition (London, 1739–45), Vol. 15

State Papers of King Henry the Eighth, 11 vols (London, 1830–52)

The Statutes of the Realm, 11 vols (London, 1817), Vol. III [*SoR*]

STOW, JOHN, *The Annales, or, General Chronicle of London* (London, 1615)

STRYPE, JOHN, *Ecclesiastical Memorials, Relating Chiefly to Religion, and
    the Reformation* . . . *under Henry VIII, King Edward VI and Queen
    Mary I*, 3 vols (London, 1822) [*EM*]

TYTLER, P.F. (ed.), *England under the Reigns of Edward VI and Mary,
    etc.*, 2 vols (London, 1839)

WRIOTHESLEY, CHARLES, *A Chronicle of England During the Reigns of the Tudors, From AD 1485 to 1559*, edited by William Douglas Hamilton, Vol. I (London, 1875)

SECONDARY SOURCES

ARMSTRONG, C.D.C., "English Catholicism Rethought?," *Journal of Ecclesiastical History*, Vol. LIV (2003): pp. 717–26

BALDWIN SMITH, LACEY, "The Last Will and Testament of Henry VIII: A Question of Perspective," *Journal of British Studies*, Vol 2, No. 1 (1962): pp. 14–27

———, "Henry VIII and the Protestant Triumph," *American Historical Review*, Vol. 71 (1966): pp. 1237–64

———, *Henry VIII: The Mask of Royalty* (London, 1971)

BEEM, CHARLES, "Have not wee a noble kynge? The Minority of Edward VI," in *The Royal Minorities of Medieval and Early Modern England*, edited by Beem (New York, 2008)

BERNARD, G. W., *The King's Reformation: Henry VIII and the Remaking of the English Church* (New Haven, Conn., and London, 2005)

BINDOFF, S. T., *Tudor England* (London, 1964)

———(ed.), *The History of Parliament: The House of Commons 1509–1558* (London, 1982)

BRIGDEN, SUSAN, "Henry Howard, Earl of Surrey and the 'Conjured League,'" *Historical Journal*, Vol. 37, No. 3 (1994): pp. 507–37

———, *New Worlds, Lost Worlds: The Rule of the Tudors, 1485–1603* (London, 2000)

CHILDS, JESSIE, *Henry VIII's Last Victim: The Life and Times of Henry Howard, Earl of Surrey* (London, 2006)

COLLINSON, PATRICK, "John Foxe as Historian," in *The Unabridged Acts and Monuments Online* [*TAMO*] (1576 edition; HRI Online Publications, Sheffield, 2011): www.johnfoxe.org

DODD, GWILYM, "Richard II and the Fiction of Majority Rule," in *The Royal Minorities of Medieval and Early Modern England*, edited by Charles Beem (New York, 2008)

ELTON, G. R., *Henry VIII: An Essay in Revision* (London, 1962)

———, *Reform and Reformation* (London, 1977)

FREEMAN, THOMAS S., "One Survived: The Account of Katherine Parr in Foxe's 'Book of Martyrs,'" in *Henry VIII and the Court: Art, Politics and Performance*, edited by Thomas Betteridge and Suzannah Lipscomb (Farnham, Surrey, 2013)

GAMMON, SAMUEL RHEA, *Statesman and Schemer: William, First Lord Paget, Tudor Minister* (Newton Abbot, Devon, 1973)

GIBBONS, GEOFFREY, *The Political Career of Thomas Wriothesley, First Earl of Southampton, 1505–1550, Henry VIII's Last Chancellor* (Lewiston, N.Y., 2001)

GRIFFITHS, R. A., "The Minority of Henry VI, King of England and of France," in *The Royal Minorities of Medieval and Early Modern England*, edited by Charles Beem (New York, 2008)

GUY, JOHN, *Tudor England* (Oxford, 1988)

———, *My Heart is My Own: The Life of Mary Queen of Scots* (London, 2004)

HAMILTON, DAKOTA L., "The Household of Queen Katherine Parr" (unpublished D.Phil. thesis, University of Oxford, 1992)

Heal, F. M., *Of Prelates and Princes* (Cambridge, 1980)

HICKERSON, MEGAN L., "'Ways of Lying': Anne Askew and the *Examinations*," *Gender & History*, Vol. 18, No. 1 (2006): pp. 50–65

Hicks, Michael, "A Story of Failure: The Minority of Edward V," in *The Royal Minorities of Medieval and Early Modern England*, edited by Charles Beem (New York, 2008)

HOAK, DALE, *The King's Council in the Reign of Edward VI* (Cambridge, 1976)

HOULBROOKE, R. A., "Debate: Henry VIII's Wills: A Comment," *Historical Journal*, Vol. 37, No. 4 (1994): pp. 891–9

HUTCHINSON, ROBERT, *The Last Days of Henry VIII* (London, 2005)

IVES, ERIC W., "Henry VIII's Will: A Forensic Conundrum," *Historical Journal*, Vol. 35, No. 4 (1992): pp. 779–804

————, "Henry VIII's Will: The Protectorate Provisions of 1546–7," *Historical Journal*, Vol. 37, No. 4 (1994): pp. 901–14

————, *Lady Jane Grey: A Tudor Mystery* (Chichester, 2009)

JAMES, SUSAN E., *Kateryn Parr: The Making of a Queen* (Farnham, Surrey, 1999)

JORDAN, W. K., *Edward VI: The Young King* (London, 1968)

LEVINE, MORTIMER, "The Last Will and Testament of Henry VIII: A Reappraisal Appraised," *Historian*, Vol. 26, No. 4 (1964): pp. 471–85

————, "Henry VIII's Use of His Spiritual and Temporal Jurisdictions in His Great Causes of Matrimony, Legitimacy and Succession," *Historical Journal*, Vol. 10, No. 1 (1967): pp. 3–10

LIPSCOMB, SUZANNAH, *1536: The Year That Changed Henry VIII* (Oxford, 2009)

LOACH, JENNIFER, "The Function of Ceremonial in the Reign of Henry VIII," *Past and Present*, Vol. CXLII (1994): pp. 43–68

————, *Edward VI*, edited by George Bernard and Penry Williams (New Haven, Conn., and London, 1999)

LOADES, DAVID, *John Dudley, Duke of Northumberland 1504–1553* (Oxford, 1996)

LOCKYER, ROGER, *Tudor and Stuart Britain* (New York, 1964)

MACCULLOCH, DIARMAID, *Thomas Cranmer: A Life* (New Haven, Conn., and London, 1996)

————, *Tudor Church Militant: Edward VI and the Protestant Reformation* (London, 1999)

MARSHALL, PETER, "Death" (online article for Royal Historic Palaces, Hampton Court): www.hrp.org.uk/ HamptonCourtPalace/stories/palacehighlights/ AlivingTudorworld/AllaboutHenryVIII

————, "Mumpsimus and Sumpsimus," in his *Religious Identities in Henry VIII's England* (Aldershot, 2006)

MILLER, HELEN, "Henry VIII's Unwritten Will: Grants of Lands and Honours in 1547," in *Wealth and Power in Tudor England*, edited by E. W. Ives *et al.* (London, 1978)

MULLER, J. A., *Stephen Gardiner and the Tudor Reaction* (London, 1926)

PAUL, JOANNE, "Counsel and Command in English Political Thought, 1485–1651," unpublished PhD thesis (Queen Mary, University of London, 2013)

POLLARD, A. F., *England Under Protector Somerset: An Essay* (London, 1900)

REDWORTH, GLYN, *In Defence of the Church Catholic: The Life of Stephen Gardiner* (Oxford, 1990)

RYRIE, ALEC, *The Gospel and Henry VIII: Evangelicals in the Early English Reformation* (Cambridge, 2003)

SCARISBRICK, J. J., *Henry VIII* (New Haven, Conn., 1968)

SKIDMORE, CHRIS, *Edward VI: The Lost King of England* (London, 2007)

STARKEY, DAVID, "Court and Government," in *Revolution Reassessed*, edited by C. Coleman and D. Starkey (Oxford, 1986)

———(ed.), *Rivals in Power: Lives and Letters of the Great Tudor Dynasties* (London, 1990)

———, *The Reign of Henry VIII: Personalities and Politics* (London, 1995 edition

———, *Six Wives: The Queens of Henry VIII* (London, 2003)

———, (ed.), with Alasdair Hawkyard and Philip Ward, *The Inventory of King Henry VIII: The Transcript* (London 1998)

STURGE, CHARLES, *Cuthbert Tunstal: Churchman, Scholar, Statesman, Administrator* (London, 1938)

WABUDA, SUSAN, "Shaxton, Nicholas (*c.*1485–1556), entry in *Oxford Dictionary of National Biography* [*ODNB*] (published in print and online 2004): www.oxforddnb.com/view/article/25276

WHITELOCK, ANNA, *Mary Tudor: England's First Queen* (London, 2009)

WILLEN, DIANE, *John Russell, First Earl of Bedford: One of the King's Men* (London, 1981)

WOODING, LUCY, *Henry VIII* (Abingdon, Oxfordshire, 2009)

Acknowledgments

I am particularly indebted to the excellent work of Professor Eric Ives on Henry VIII's will. I am grateful to the staff of the London Library, the British Library, the National Archives, and the Bodleian Library, who have been so kind in helping me locate sources.

I am thankful, too, for the support I have received from my colleagues and students at New College of the Humanities, particularly from Dr. Hannah Dawson, Dr. Lars Kjaer, Dr. Joanne Paul, and Professor Anthony Grayling. My student Paula Erizanu acted as a research assistant for me in the early stages of this book, and her bibliographic research was invaluable. Thank you to all fellow members of the Ottoline Club, our interdisciplinary faculty club, for their helpful comments on my early paper on this material, and to Dr. David Mitchell for the invitation to present my research. Thank you, too, to my second-year students who endured digressions into the subject of the will during their Michaelmas 2014 tutorials on the Tudors.

Personally, I want to thank Marie-Noëlle Raynal-Bechetoille and Philippe Raynal for creating such a wonderful atmosphere in which to write; Suzanne Phillips and Sarah Broughton for their massive practical help and encouragement as I started out writing; and my parents, Nick and Marguerite Lipscomb, for their great support and hands-on help. Thank you, also, to all my friends for encouragement, companionship, and welcome distraction, but especially to Hannah Dawson, Thomas Leveritt, Josh Dell, and Simon Schama.

Finally, I particularly want to thank my dear friend Dan Jones, who cajoled, encouraged, bullied, and inspired me into writing this.

SUZANNAH LIPSCOMB

Index